Praise for *Expec...*

With raw honesty, wit, and bi... heart to lean upon God's sus... ...g p... ...and love in mother-hood—in everyday challenges from cleaning up a shattered bowl of whipped cream or facing a fresh day after a sleepless night, to the larger pain of navigating unexpected loss. Prepare to worship the Lord in both the difficult and delightful moments as a mom as you read *Expect Something Beautiful*. You'll treasure this book!

HEATHER HOLLEMAN, author of *Seated with Christ: Living Freely in a Culture of Comparison*

This is the book I wish I had in hand when raising my kids. Laura is the perfect mentor to encourage you in the sometimes-daunting assignment of being a mother. Her enthusiasm for motherhood, and for the One who gives us the good gift of children, is contagious. You'll be inspired and challenged as you work your way through these pages.

MARY A. KASSIAN, Bible teacher, author, *Girls Gone Wise* and *The Right Kind of Strong*

Laura blends a delightful gift for storytelling and a dose of levity with sound biblical wisdom. *Expect Something Beautiful* will encourage new and seasoned mamas alike to embrace and enjoy the gifts of motherhood and to experience the enabling grace of Christ for this challenging calling.

NANCY DEMOSS WOLGEMUTH, author; Revive Our Hearts founder and Bible teacher

The gap between what we expect motherhood to be and what we experience can often leave us frustrated and disappointed. *Expect Something Beautiful* lifts our gaze from the mundane to the majestic and invites us to realign our expectations through His Word. You can expect this book to be a gracious gospel classroom taught by a fellow mom about the sacred stewardship of motherhood.

KAREN HODGE, Coordinator of Women's Ministries for the Presbyterian Church in America (PCA) and coauthor of *Transformed: Life-taker to Life-giver* and *Life-giving Leadership*

Laura Booz offers an abundant depiction of the reality of God's own self-giving, attentive—and even, yes, mothering—presence to those who sojourn in the short years and long days of the mothering vocation. Mindful of all the longing and loss, the daily victories and failures, her book is full of joy, discovery, encouragement, and wise paths of hope.

LAURA M. FABRYCKY, author of *Keys to Bonhoeffer's Haus: Exploring the World and Wisdom of Dietrich Bonhoeffer*

Motherhood is filled with expectations, both for ourselves and our children. But what can we expect from God? In *Expect Something Beautiful*, Laura Booz paints a beautiful picture of the work God is doing in and through us as we mother our children. We can expect beautiful things—whether we are cleaning up the latest spills, solving sibling spats, or instructing hearts in the Word of God. This gospel-saturated book provides encouragement for every mother's heart.

CHRISTINA FOX, author of *Idols of a Mother's Heart* and *Sufficient Hope: Gospel Meditations and Prayers for Moms*

As a mom of four who's walked many difficult roads in motherhood, I found the pages of this book to be beautifully written, intensely practical, and biblically rich. Rather than portraying an unrealistic pursuit of perfection, Laura walks alongside us to show that it's in the very messes, chaos, and challenges of motherhood that we can come to truly expect something beautiful.

SARAH WALTON, coauthor of *Hope When It Hurts* and *Together Through the Storms*

I wept . . . sobbed, actually . . . through the second half of the book. It was like a mirror, and in my reflection I saw a mother whose gentleness and kindness was largely conditional, as if those traits were something my children earned. But Laura's teaching doesn't just uncover the hard things. She swiftly takes the reader to a place of hope for change and new life for both the woman and the child. This book has literally transformed the way I view motherhood, and I couldn't be more grateful.

JANET MYLIN, author of *Arrows Make Terrible Crowns: How the Holy Spirit Healed My View of Motherhood*

This book will bring hope and encouragement to any mother, grandmother, or spiritual mom. Laura's captivating stories of her adventures in motherhood will make you laugh and cry, while her wisdom, honesty, and Christ-centered approach to parenting will inspire you to look to God and His sufficiency in your times of need.

NICOLE FURNO, writer, Bible teacher, mom of three

So many today fear or scorn the beautiful calling of motherhood. It is so refreshing to read Laura's book! She does not hide the struggles inherent to this role, but she beautifully highlights the sure help, abundant grace, and expectant hope mothers receive from Jesus. Mothers are not alone. They are seen, cared for, and strengthened by their Savior as they live this beautiful and rewarding calling of motherhood. A must-read for every mom!

LAURA GONZALEZ DE CHAVEZ, Director of Aviva Nuestros Corazones, the Spanish outreach of Revive Our Hearts

With obvious joy in Jesus Christ, Laura has written a faithful, biblical testament to God's goodness in motherhood through *Expect Something Beautiful*. I hope this practical book will prompt you to serve the Lord Jesus with gladness and bask in His grace even as you serve your precious little ones.

KRISTEN WETHERELL, author of *Humble Moms* and *Fight Your Fears*

For any mom who is feeling overlooked, overtired, or simply underwhelmed by the quotidian work of her days, *Expect Something Beautiful* speaks a gracious and encouraging word. Pick it up, and delight again in the dignity of motherhood, and the remarkable school it can be for discipleship and transformation.

SARAH DAHL, creator and host of *We Wonder*

I wasn't even through the intro before I struck gold. Laura is the mentor you've always wanted: sharing transparently from her own sixteen-year motherhood journey, cheering you on in yours, and pointing you to the beauty of God. *Expect Something Beautiful* is inspiring, worshipful, Scripture-saturated, and practical. May it bless your heart as it did mine.

PAULA (HENDRICKS) MARSTELLER, author of *Confessions of a Boy-Crazy Girl*, mom of a preschooler and a toddler

There is something both fierce and humble about Laura's voice, for she has an old kind of commitment to her chosen path, the kind you might find in a medieval monastic. But at the same time, she is brimming over with compassion for the challenges (both yours and hers) of doubt, struggle, fatigue, and self-recrimination. Come to this book for the lovely prose, for the wise, gentle, and often quite practical advice, but most of all for the rare opportunity to transform your daily motherhood into a joyful vocation.

AMY ALZNAUER, coauthor of *Love & Salt,* and *The Strange Birds of Flannery O'Connor*

Laura Booz has written one of the most honest, relatable, and beautiful books on motherhood I have ever read. Laura reminds us, when do we need the kindness of our Creator if not now? In your moments of joy and in the inevitable heartbreak, let Laura's words point you back to Jesus. She will show you how to find Him, right here.

CATHERINE MCNIEL, author of *Long Days of Small Things: Motherhood as a Spiritual Discipline*

EXPECT SOMETHING

Beautiful

FINDING GOD'S GOOD GIFTS IN MOTHERHOOD

LAURA BOOZ

MOODY PUBLISHERS
CHICAGO

© 2021 by
LAURA BOOZ

Some content has been adapted from material previously published by the author online.

Scripture quotations, unless otherwise noted, are taken from the ESV® Bible (The Holy Bible, English Standard Version®), copyright © 2001 by Crossway, a publishing ministry of Good News Publishers. Used by permission. All rights reserved.

Scripture quotations marked (NIV) are taken from the Holy Bible, New International Version®, NIV®. Copyright © 1973, 1978, 1984, 2011 by Biblica, Inc.™ Used by permission of Zondervan. All rights reserved worldwide. www.zondervan.com The "NIV" and "New International Version" are trademarks registered in the United States Patent and Trademark Office by Biblica, Inc.

Scripture quotations marked KJV are from the King James Version.

All emphasis in Scripture quotations has been added.

Edited by Pamela Joy Pugh
Interior design: Kaylee Lockenour and Erik M. Peterson
Cover design: Kaylee Lockenour
Cover image of gift box copyright © 2020 by Golubovy / Shutterstock (1755754802). All rights reserved.
Author photo: Samantha Loucks

Library of Congress Cataloging-in-Publication Data

Names: Booz, Laura, author.
Title: Expect something beautiful : finding God's good gifts in motherhood
  / Laura Booz.
Description: Chicago : Moody Publishers, [2021] | Includes bibliographical
  references. | Summary: "Motherhood makes high demands. Will you pour out
  your life for your children while getting little in return? No, you can
  expect something truly beautiful out of motherhood. Behind all the
  giving that mothers do is the receiving of something special"-- Provided
  by publisher.
Identifiers: LCCN 2021022844 | ISBN 9780802424198 (paperback) | ISBN
  9780802499851 (ebook)
Subjects: LCSH: Motherhood--Religious aspects--Christianity. |
  Mothers--Religious life. | BISAC: RELIGION / Christian Living /
  Parenting | RELIGION / Christian Living / Women's Interests
Classification: LCC BV4529.18 .B65 2021 | DDC 248.8/431--dc23
LC record available at https://lccn.loc.gov/20210228444

Originally delivered by fleets of horse-drawn wagons, the affordable paperbacks from D. L. Moody's publishing house resourced the church and served everyday people. Now, after more than 125 years of publishing and ministry, Moody Publishers' mission remains the same— even if our delivery systems have changed a bit. For more information on other books (and resources) created from a biblical perspective, go to www.moodypublishers.com or write to:

Moody Publishers
820 N. LaSalle Boulevard
Chicago, IL 60610

1 3 5 7 9 10 8 6 4 2

Printed in the United States of America

TO MY CHILDREN

CONTENTS

SOMETIMES
I WONDER . . .

*What if I got to the end of my day and felt
like I accomplished something?*

*What if I didn't feel like I had been derailed
and distracted all day?*

*What if I knew for a fact that my time
and energy went toward something
constructive?*

Wouldn't that be nice? Do you ever feel the same way?

Before we get started, let's link arms and remember that motherhood isn't a distraction or an inconvenience. It isn't a side gig or a job. Motherhood is a relationship with a person—handpicked by God—for us to love. Cultivating this relationship and meeting our child's needs is hard work, but it's always worthwhile. I wonder . . . what if we anticipated the tasks ahead in our day, writing them out like a God-given mission statement? It might help us think more accurately about our calling as moms and feel satisfied with the work we do every day to nurture our children. In the end, maybe we'll see what God sees: the makings of a beautiful relationship.

Here's a sample:

Today . . .
I will open the blinds to let the sunshine in.
I will hug my child
and fill a hungry belly.
I will clean a little bottom,
wash a little face,
and hold two little hands.

Today . . .
I will dress someone,
carry someone,
and walk alongside.
I will teach,
and play,
and sing.

Today . . .
I will repeat myself a dozen times
and answer a dozen questions.

I will calm chaos,
address meanness,
and encourage kindness.
I will look for growth
and treasure it.

Today . . .
someone will yell for help passionately—urgently.
I will run to the rescue.
Sometimes I'll discover a legitimate emergency,
but most of the time, it will be the smallest complaint that will
    melt with a kiss.
I will clean up spills,
fix something that's broken,
find something that's lost,
and buy something that's needed.
I will uphold boundaries and keep schedules.
I will wake someone who is sleeping
and help someone sleep who is wakeful.

Today . . .
I'll notice more reasons to smile
and stumble upon reasons to cry.
I will wrestle irritability,
spar with self-pity,
sprint from temptation,
and win (sometimes).

When I fall, I'll fall on grace.

Today...
I will say, "I am sorry,"
and "I forgive you,"
and "I choose you."

Today...
my work as a mother will resemble God's work as our heavenly Father.
My occupation is His occupation;
my mission, His own.

And today...
if this is all I accomplish,
I will fall asleep feeling quite satisfied indeed.

Today...
I will do these anticipated tasks because God Himself wakes me up in the morning, feeds me with the Living Bread, cheers me on, and runs to my rescue when I call for help.

May these words and those ahead in this book encourage you as you embrace what you can expect from God's good hand—something beautiful. Now, let's get started!

PART ONE

THE ESSENTIALS

Seek the LORD and his strength;
seek his presence continually!

—*Psalm 105:4*

MOTHERHOOD— WHAT'S IN IT FOR YOU?

Let the favor of the Lord our God be upon us,
and establish the work of our hands upon us;
yes, establish the work of our hands!

—PSALM 90:17

EXPECT GOD TO CARE ABOUT WHO YOU ARE BECOMING

The ambulance barreled down the highway toward the nearest NICU. I lay inside on a gurney—only seven months pregnant—

breathing through contractions. My heart was beating fast and my thoughts swirled with confusion. *What was going on?* Until now, everything had gone according to plan. The pregnancy book on my nightstand had been a comforting resource: I regularly reviewed its step-by-step predictions about what was happening in my body and to my baby. Morning sickness? Check. Charlie horses? Check. Kicks and flutters? Check, check. The book seemed accurate until, in a blink, it became completely irrelevant.

My list of "what to expect in pregnancy" did not include a frantic phone call to my family or a conversation with the hospital chaplain about the possibility of a high-risk birth. It did not include a sudden and overwhelming fear of the unknown. I was quickly learning that one of the only things a woman can truly expect in motherhood is unpredictability.

Only four years earlier, my husband and I had gone out on our first date. I wish I could go back in time and see us sitting across from each other at the steak house, me in a lavender sweater and Ryan in a button-down. We were so young. At the time, I was in graduate school and Ryan was forging ahead in his career. We exchanged the normal pleasantries about work, friends, and hobbies and then, so as not to waste Ryan's time or mine, I told him that I wanted to be a mom someday. The waiter had just delivered our surf and turf platters when I added, "And I want *six kids.*" Ryan paused, fork poised in midair. He raised his eyebrows and then, diving into his steak, said that he only wanted *two kids.* You'd think we would've called it a night and gone our separate ways. But the rest of the date went so well that, despite our significant life plan disparity, we got married eighteen months later.

And suddenly, there I was, after three years of marriage—the whirlwind ambulance ride, several weeks of bed rest, and an epic delivery that caused even the nurses to shudder—holding our first child. I lay in the hospital bed, just grateful to be alive. I looked at Ryan and murmured, "Did I say *six kids*? I meant *one kid*. One precious child, and here she is." Ryan took one look at that sweet baby girl and said, "Did I say *two kids*? I'll meet you at *four*."

Well, you know how that goes. We talked big and dreamed big and had no idea what God had in store for us.

OUR EXPECTATIONS REALLY MATTER

From beginning to end, our expectations about motherhood matter. They shape what we look for, what we fight for, and what we cherish along the way. Some expectations must be held lightly, for they can be overturned in a moment. Other expectations must be held tightly, for they are as good as done. We want to make sure we know the difference.

You may ask, "What did you expect of motherhood?" Maybe I expected love. Or happiness. If I dig a little deeper, maybe I expected the joy of introducing a child to Jesus, or raising a good citizen or a top student. To be honest, for all my daydreaming, I don't know what I expected. Motherhood has been one big surprise for me. For starters, I've been completely blindsided by the love that invades a mother's heart and the way she will do anything for her child's well-being. I've been stunned by the female body and how it sustains life—sometimes seamlessly, other times with significant effort. I've been shocked by the amount of laundry, noise, band-aids, giggles, hugs, and awe a child brings into a woman's life. Most of all, I have been astonished by the way God pursues a woman through motherhood and makes her more like Jesus.

I've wrestled with the cost of motherhood. I've wondered, **Am I losing myself? Am I compromising my career and squandering my potential? Do my unseen sacrifices amount to anything?**

(Spoiler alert!) My husband, Ryan, and I do have six children, ranging in age from two to sixteen. They are great kids who love to laugh, explore, and create. They're also normal kids who struggle with arguing, disobedience, and the works. But they forgive easily and are easy to forgive. We live on a beautiful little farm in central Pennsylvania where we raise chickens, honeybees, and midsummer tomatoes. We toast mountain pies on the campfire and read books under the maple trees. Sometimes it feels like a dream. We have so much to be grateful for. But life is not all roses. Life—for everyone—is replete with thorns. Any amount of growth comes from a mixture of joy and sorrow. Thanks be to God for His presence in all things.

In those early days of first dates and big dreams, I certainly didn't expect that I would feel overworked and overlooked as a mom, but I have sometimes. This has been an unwelcome surprise.

I've wrestled with the cost of motherhood. I've wondered, *Am I losing myself? Am I compromising my career and squandering my potential? Do my unseen sacrifices amount to anything?* Have you ever wondered these things? I think all moms do. We know that motherhood is good for children and even good for civilization, but at the heart of our glorious calling, most of us ask, "Is motherhood good for me?"

Over the past sixteen years, God has assured me that, yes, motherhood is indeed good for me—and for every mom. He has formed treasures in me through the desert land of infertility and the lush pastures of raising children; in the valley of stillbirth and the mountaintop of healthy full-term deliveries; and in the everyday work and play. Motherhood has never been easy, but God has been faithful to His promises and has answered impossible prayers.

I have seen His hand at work in other moms too. The story is always the same: as a woman walks with God through motherhood, He transforms her into a person who clings to Him and sees people the way He does. To see this at work is the most beautiful thing in the world. It's a story worth telling.

This is your story too. Whether motherhood feels exciting or exhausting, God is with you. Whether your own mother nourished you or neglected you, God is redeeming your story. He sees you and wants to win your heart. (Motherhood hasn't changed that one bit.) In fact, He is forming treasures in you as you care for your child. He is giving you ironclad trust in His promises, bravery in the face of fear, and the opportunity to worship Him in the big moments and the mundane. These treasures are not immediate. They emerge through joy and sorrow, victory and defeat. They come through the slow, steady relationship between a woman and her Maker, forged in the Word, the church, and each moment in between.

God will not give up on you or leave you halfway. He will complete the good work He started in you (Phil. 1:6). Of course, He would do this whether or not you are a mother. But if you are a mother, He will purposefully use motherhood to draw you to Himself, form Christ in you, and give you hope.

WHAT YOU CAN EXPECT FROM THIS BOOK

I want to let you know up front that I love motherhood. I love being with my kids and seeing them grow. Motherhood is one of the few things that gets top real estate in my brain. You may not love motherhood—not every woman does—so I hope you can see me as a friend who is simply sharing what she has gathered. It's the least I could do: after all, I benefit from women who love important areas of life that barely show up in my brain at all (like cooking and finances, for instance).

You may or may not be like me, and your child may or may not be like mine, but my goal in writing this book is not to promote my personality or my parenting preferences. My goal is to consider biblical truths that apply to every mom and every child in every circumstance. I wouldn't write a book about motherhood if I couldn't count on the Word of God to cast a vision for each one of us who is uniquely created and unconditionally loved by our heavenly Father.

Part One of *Expect Something Beautiful* explores the essential Christian disciplines such as Bible reading and prayer that will help you thrive in motherhood. If you are new to Christianity, you may be curious about how these practices will benefit you. I'll try to offer some helpful answers. If you are a Christian, you probably love these aspects of the faith, but you may be wondering how to incorporate them into your life as a mom. I'm wondering too. Together, we'll explore mom-friendly opportunities to enjoy them. We'll need these essentials of motherhood in order to receive the other gifts God has in store for us.

I hope this book helps us sort out our expectations and find every reason to expect something beautiful.

In Part Two, we'll unwrap ten more gifts, all given to us freely through Jesus. These chapters focus on different aspects of the fruit of the Spirit from Galatians 5, like peace in the ups and downs, patience in trial, and self-control to go the distance.

Only now, with sixteen years of motherhood under my belt, am I beginning to understand the things a woman can expect from motherhood, especially the things she can really, truly count on. This book is a look back over what I've learned in motherhood so far, with the hope of figuring out what you and I can hold on to for the future. Along the way, I'll share personal stories and beloved Scriptures to strengthen us in our motherhood journey, no matter where we are along the way. I hope this book helps us sort out our expectations and find every reason to expect something beautiful.

A NOTE TO NEW MOMS

You are dear to my heart. When I think of you, the word *potential* comes to mind. I imagine you—your hands clasped in prayer as you long to be pregnant, or a palm resting on your growing womb, or adoption papers in hand, or an infant nestled in your arms, or a toddler squirming out of your arms—and I see a world of potential in you: potential love, surrender, grit, trust, and gratitude. God has filled you to the brim with life. He will be your all-in-all, upholding the massive weight of glory He has placed inside you. Motherhood will make sense when you see it through this lens.

RECEIVING GOD'S GIFT OF MOTHERHOOD

Something to cherish:
I thank my God in all my remembrance of you, always in every prayer of mine for you all making my prayer with joy, because of your partnership in the gospel from the first day until now. And I am sure of this, that he who began a good work in you will bring it to completion at the day of Jesus Christ. It is right for me to feel this way about you all, because I hold you in my heart, for you are all partakers with me of grace. Philippians 1:3–7

Something to sing:
"All That Is to Come" by Christy Nockels

Something to read:
Every Moment Holy by Douglas Kaine McKelvey

Something to consider:

- Which of my expectations about motherhood would God like me to hold lightly? Which would He like me to hold tightly for the future?

- Can I ask God to sift my expectations until only His remain?

- How is God pursuing me even now?

MY PRAYER FOR YOU: *May your mind be sharpened by thoughts of what truly matters. May your heart be fortified with love for God and people, especially for your child. May you hunger for God until you want what He wants more than anything else in the world. May fellowship with Christ and Christlikeness become your great delight as you discover that Jesus is the gift of motherhood. And may God give you every reason to thank Him for today and look forward to tomorrow.*

Chapter 1

JESUS BY YOUR SIDE

If you want to get warm you must stand
near the fire: if you want to be wet you
must get into the water. If you want joy,
power, peace, eternal life,
you must get close to, or even into,
the thing that has them.[1]

—C. S. LEWIS, *MERE CHRISTIANITY*

EXPECT JESUS TO BE YOUR DEAREST FRIEND

What's your earliest memory of motherhood? Mine goes back to my mom. She opened the blinds to let the sunshine in, cheered for me at swim meets, hosted fun birthday parties, and made amazing Philly cheesesteaks—but the most important thing she did was introduce me to Jesus. You could see glimpses of it yourself in a rickety, circa-1980s home video. I'm a curly-haired toddler wearing an orange jacket with the hood cinched around my chubby cheeks. My mom is kneeling next to me, holding a microphone as I sing an old gospel chorus, "Mine, mine, mine, Jesus is mine. Mine in the morning, mine in the evening." She taught me this song and many others like it. She read Bible stories to me and prayed for me.

Mom says I was two-and-a-half years old when I sat in the kitchen and said, "Last night when I was in bed, Jesus came into my heart." Although a toddler's confession of faith may not be the most reliable thing in the world, I believe mine was genuine because, forty years later, I can honestly say that Jesus has been my Lord and Savior ever since. Though I have often strayed from Him, He has faithfully pursued me. I've always sensed Him carrying me close to His heart.

HOW DO WE KNOW WE'RE DOING IT RIGHT?

As a child, I loved to play "mommy." I would gather my dolls on my lap and teach them Bible stories. I'd feed them plastic peas with a tiny plastic spoon and tuck them into their doll beds. Motherhood seemed simple and satisfying. Now that I am the mother of real, live children, I'm learning that motherhood is far more complex than I thought it would be. For example, I teach my children songs about Jesus and we talk about His love, but I cannot make them lay hold of Him. I work hard to clothe and feed them, but they don't eat their peas as readily as my dolls did.

I tuck them into bed, tell them stories, rub their backs, and army crawl out of their rooms only to see them pop out of bed, bright-eyed and ready for an all-nighter. *What to do?*

Although raising a child can be deeply satisfying, it sure does come with never-ending unknowns. How do we know we're doing it right? What's best for these little people whom we love so much? And how can we maintain some sense of personhood even when we're completely immersed in the daily work of caring for our kids?

When I feel overwhelmed, this verse gives me peace. When I feel sidelined, this verse assures me I am not. When I wonder if God cares, this verse assures me that He does.

Sometimes I wonder if God wants me to figure out a way to faithfully raise my children while maximizing my potential, multiplying my talents, and doing ministry work outside our home. I wonder if I am supposed to "do it all," and when I fail miserably (which I do), it's simply because I'm too lazy, disorganized, or selfish. Or do I indulge my children with too much attention when I should be doing more outside my home? Or am I too distracted and not giving my kids enough care and companionship? Sometimes I wonder if I'm just sidelined in the great walk of faith until I can get it all together.

Does God care? When He created children to be so needy and mothers to be so necessary for their survival, did He shrug off the eighteen-plus years His daughters would be thoroughly consumed by motherhood? Does He provide any help for the journey?

Whenever I'm struggling with these questions, a particular verse in the Bible answers me with unmistakable clarity. It's like a bodyguard, protecting me from discouragement. When I feel overwhelmed, this verse gives me peace. When I feel sidelined, this verse assures me I am not. When I wonder if God cares, this verse assures me that He does.

This verse has been a game changer for me in motherhood, and I think it will be for you too.

It's Isaiah 40:11.

> He will tend his flock like a shepherd;
> he will gather the lambs in his arms;
> he will carry them in his bosom,
> and gently lead those that are with young.

In this single sentence, the prophet Isaiah assures us that Jesus sees us. He cares about us. He is with us in motherhood. The better we grasp these truths, the better we can navigate the questions and doubts that come our way. We're going to explore these truths in more detail, but first we have to zoom out and take a look at Isaiah 40 for some context.

THE BIG PICTURE

Have you ever seen the conclusion of a World War II movie when Allied soldiers drive through Europe announcing that the war is over? As the soldiers work their way through war-ravaged towns with the good news, people emerge from their hiding places, blinking in astonishment, hoping life will finally be as it should: peaceful and free of fear. The villagers clear the rubble and rebuild their homes. Flowers grow. Children play. Mothers smile.

Isaiah 40 is this type of long-awaited announcement: Jerusalem's warfare will be over when the Messiah comes to pardon her iniquity and redeem her. Life will finally be as it should. People will emerge from their hiding places, no longer terrorized by sin and death. They will build their homes, knowing all is well. This announcement of peace is the longing of every human heart. No wonder God begins Isaiah 40 with the words, "Comfort, comfort my people."

Though we may content ourselves on scraps and seconds, Jesus cares for us the way a shepherd cares for the ewes. Jesus takes special care of mothers.

Isaiah goes on to describe the Messiah who will put an end to our war and give us peace. He says the Messiah is far beyond our comprehension. He is the Creator who has cupped the oceans in His palm, measured the sky with His hand, and named the stars. The entire chapter is a rousing account of the Messiah's preeminence over creation. To set up Isaiah 40:11, Isaiah writes in verse 10,

> *Behold, the Lord GOD comes with might,*
> *and his arm rules for him;*
> *behold, his reward is with him,*
> *and his recompense before him.*

From this context, we may imagine the Messiah as a fierce warrior marching victoriously over the conquered earth, but that's not how Isaiah goes on to describe Him. Instead, Isaiah says that our great victor is like a shepherd who gathers His flock around Him, holds the lambs in His arms, and gently leads the mama ewes. On this side of redemptive history, we understand that Jesus is the Shepherd, our children are the lambs, and you and I are the mother sheep. And we are an integral part of His victory march.

Isaiah 40:11 assures us that Jesus does not sideline mothers, nor does He deal harshly with us, expecting us to do it all. On the contrary, Jesus takes special care of mothers. It's not that we're more important or weaker than anyone else, but because we give of our very substance to nurture children made in the image of God, Jesus pulls us close to His side.

Though we may content ourselves on scraps and seconds, Jesus cares for mothers the way a shepherd cares for nursing ewes. He feeds us with the highest quality nutrient-dense food, provides an abundance of fresh water, fends off our enemies, guides us step by step in the shadowlands, and remains our closest companion.

OUR CHILDREN BELONG TO GOD

I love this portrait of Jesus as He gathers the lambs in His arms and carries them close to His heart. These lambs are our children. Take a moment to imagine your child in His strong, capable arms.

- me too -

Sometimes I forget that my children belong to Jesus. Then I recall that He has created each child and has recorded their days in His book. He thinks about them constantly and died for those who believe in Him, that they would not perish but have eternal life (John 3:16). Throughout Scripture, He advocates for children, teaching us to care about their physical and spiritual well-being. He compels us to love them dearly because they are His own.

Jesus came to us as a child Himself. Then, when He was an adult embarking on intense ministry work, Jesus welcomed children into His arms and blessed them. His fervent disciples assumed the children were inconveniencing Him, so they pushed them aside, but Jesus said, "Let the little children come to me and do not hinder them, for to such belongs the kingdom of heaven" (Matt. 19:14).

Too often, we assume that God can't possibly include "motherhood" on His list of good works. We think that motherhood is just something we must juggle while we pursue the **real** *good works.*

Here Jesus shows us the beautiful balance of engaging in the work of the kingdom and stopping everything to show the little ones how precious they are to God. You and I may hold our children close to our hearts, but what really matters is that the Lord Strong and Mighty holds them close to His.

JESUS LEADS US IN MOTHERHOOD

When God gives a woman the gift of a child, He also gives her the gift of good work. Remember the mission statement at the beginning of this book? He ordained it all, from diapers to discipling.

> *For we are his workmanship, created in Christ Jesus for good works, which God prepared beforehand, that we should walk in them.*—Ephesians 2:10

Too often, we question the value of motherhood's work. We wonder, is it enough? I want to cheer us on with a resounding "Yes!" The stuff of motherhood is at the heart and soul of our faith: as moms, we literally feed the hungry, clothe the naked, and give the thirsty something to drink. Jesus said, "As you did it to one of the least of these my brothers, you did it to me" (Matt. 25:40). On top of that, motherhood includes the good work of entrusting our children into God's hands and pointing them to Jesus every chance we get. We equip our children for the good works that God has planned for them to do, and we strengthen them with wisdom and love. Day after day, we work to build a home life that—in some miraculous way—provides a tangible picture of the family of God.

There's no doubt about it: the work of motherhood is profoundly good. By this point, you may actually feel a bit intimidated by the magnitude of your calling to be a mom. Be encouraged by Paul David Tripp who writes, God "is not so unwise, unkind, or unfaithful as to ever call us to a task without enabling us to do it."[2] Remember, we are not alone in this. God will lead us one step at a time. Our job is to follow Him.

Christians often talk about following Jesus, but what does it really mean? Why do we follow Jesus? And where is He leading us? Is He a tour guide who recommends wholesome family activities? Is He a life coach who helps us maximize our potential and find true happiness? Is He a consultant who answers our questions about baby food, temper tantrums, and social media? In order to get the most out of motherhood, we have to figure out what it really means to follow Jesus.

The next section answers these questions. It may seem a bit academic, but I can assure you that there is nothing more practical for our everyday life. So, pour yourself a tall glass of water and get ready to consider some deep foundational truths about Jesus and your life as a mom.

Jesus leads us out of sin. Jesus said He came to earth, "to seek and to save the lost" (Luke 19:10). His mission in becoming a man, dying on a cross, and being raised from the grave was to rescue us from sin, restore our relationship with God, and give us eternal life. He elaborated on His mission when He said,

> *"The Spirit of the Lord is upon me,*
> *because he has anointed me*
> *to proclaim good news to the poor.*
> *He has sent me to proclaim liberty to the captives*
> *and recovering of sight to the blind,*

to set at liberty those who are oppressed,
to proclaim the year of the Lord's favor."—Luke 4:18–19

This passage illuminates what Jesus did and what He is still doing as the Savior of the world. Now seated at the right hand of God the Father in heaven, Jesus is still proclaiming the good news, releasing captives, recovering sight, and rescuing oppressed people through the power of His Holy Spirit and the ministry of His church. He wants to lead us and our kids out of sin so that we may experience abundant life too. He wants to replace our hearts of stone with hearts of flesh.

Jesus leads us to be like Him. Motherhood has a way of helping us see our desperation for certain qualities we can't muster up on our own. We can't be perfect moms, no matter how hard we try. Thankfully, Jesus wants our parenting to overflow from Him so that, as we walk with Him through life, we will become more and more like Him. And not just so we can become better parents, but so we can become His holy bride.

> *Christ loved the church and gave himself up for her, that he might sanctify her, having cleansed her by the washing of water with the word, so that he might present the church to himself in splendor, without spot or wrinkle or any such thing, that she might be holy and without blemish.*
> —Ephesians 5:25–27

Jesus leads us to make disciples. Before Jesus ascended to heaven, He gathered His disciples and said,

"Go therefore and make disciples of all nations, baptizing them in the name of the Father and of the Son and of the Holy Spirit, teaching them to observe all that I have commanded you. And behold, I am with you always, to the end of the age."
—Matthew 28:19–20

He was calling all His disciples—including you and me—to work alongside Him in bringing His kingdom to earth. Our children are our dearest and closest "nation." Jesus wants them to hear His Word and believe in His name. He will always lead us to teach our kids about God, to pray for them, and to worship God with them. He will always lead us to live vibrantly, full of His glory.

Jesus leads us home. Our twenty-first-century lives, between the first and second coming of Christ, mirror the way God rescued the Israelites from slavery in Egypt, led them through the wilderness for forty years, and brought them home to the promised land.

On a much grander scale, Jesus has rescued us from slavery to sin and is leading us through the wilderness of this sinful world to our eternal home, our promised land. In fact, when Jesus said, "I am the light of the world. Whoever follows me will not walk in darkness, but will have the light of life" (John 8:12), He was referring to the way God led the Israelites through the wilderness as a bright cloud by day and a pillar of fire by night. Jesus is our pillar of light. He is on the move, leading us toward eternity.

I often get shortsighted and forget to look forward to eternity. Because "each day has enough trouble of its own," I tend to focus my energy on getting through the day, but Jesus said not

Every day, Jesus is working through motherhood to prepare us—and our children—for heaven.

to "worry about tomorrow" (Matt. 6:34 NIV); He didn't say, "Don't think about tomorrow." In fact, as we follow Jesus through this wilderness, we must think about our magnificent, soul-satisfying, everything-as-it-should-be *tomorrow*. In every quotidian task, we are stepping forward to heaven. This heaven:

> *Behold, a great multitude that no one could number, from every nation, from all tribes and peoples and languages, standing before the throne and before the Lamb, clothed in white robes, with palm branches in their hands, and crying out with a loud voice, "Salvation belongs to our God who sits on the throne, and to the Lamb!"—Revelation 7:9–10*

And this:

> *"Behold, the dwelling place of God is with man. He will dwell with them, and they will be his people, and God himself will be with them as their God. He will wipe away every tear from their eyes, and death shall be no more, neither shall there be mourning, nor crying, nor pain anymore, for the former things have passed away."—Revelation 21:3–4*

Every day, Jesus is working through motherhood to prepare us—and our children—for heaven.

Yes, Jesus cares about our specific parenting decisions. Yes,

He leads us toward good choices regarding family activities, baby food, and social media. But He ultimately leads us to heaven, where we will worship Him forever with people from every nation, starting with our little tribe at home.

FOLLOWING JESUS IN MOTHERHOOD

Now that we've examined why (and where) Jesus is leading us in motherhood, it may be helpful to consider what it looks like to follow our Good Shepherd in real time.

God recently used these truths to lead me through a common motherhood struggle. Here's what happened:

The question is not "What would Jesus do?" but "What is Jesus doing?"

It was on a day when I had been harsh with my four-year-old son. I kept pushing him away in anger instead of drawing him close in love. I needed to repent and ask God for help. The next chance I got, I talked to Jesus as if He were literally walking next to me, holding my son in His arms. The question before me was not "What *would* Jesus do?" but "What *is* Jesus doing?" I wanted to know, what is Jesus doing as He holds my son close to His heart? What is Jesus doing as He gently leads me in motherhood?

Jesus is sitting down next to our heavenly Father as our perfect righteousness (Heb. 10:12–14).

He is redeeming our brokenness (Rom. 5:9–11).

He is loving us unconditionally (Rom. 8:35–39).

Jesus is inviting my son and me to approach God's throne and ask for help any time we need it (Heb. 4:16).

He is rooting out our sin and making us holy (Heb. 12:5–11).

He is sending His Spirit to convict, comfort, teach, and woo us (John 16:8).

He is working all things for His glory and our good (Rom. 8:28).

Jesus is beckoning both of us to abide in Him and to bear fruit that will last (John 15:4–5).

He is sending His angels to guard us (Ps. 91:11–12).

And, ever so faithfully, He is praying for my son to become a son of God. He is praying for me to draw close to Him and point my son in His direction (Heb. 7:25; 1 Peter 2:9–10).

I didn't come up with all the answers right then and there. In fact, my mom helped me scour the Bible in search of Jesus' footsteps so I could see where to walk and how to respond to my son. Looking back on my day, though, I can't adequately describe the way these truths transformed my motherhood. I saw my son through new eyes and could use strategies that effectively spoke to his heart and engaged his mind. The Holy Spirit brought these truths to my attention just in time to transform my coldhearted reactions into something better. Jesus helped me win my son's heart that day. I hope I never forget it.

You and I are not alone on our motherhood journey. Jesus is leading us like a shepherd one step at a time, teaching us to be like Himself, and preparing us for heaven. This is profoundly good for us and the children we love.

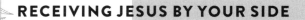

RECEIVING JESUS BY YOUR SIDE

Something to cherish:
He will tend his flock like a shepherd; he will gather the lambs in his arms; he will carry them in his bosom, and gently lead those that are with young.—Isaiah 40:11

Something to sing:
"Jesus, See the Traveler" by Sara Groves

Something to read:
Long Days of Small Things by Catherine McNiel

Something to consider:

- In what ways has mothering been good for me? How has it been hard for me?

- In what ways have I felt God gently lead me?

- In what areas of mothering do I need to seek the Lord's care and leadership? *Patience*

MY PRAYER FOR YOU: *May you receive the gift of motherhood with open arms as you draw close to Jesus and become more like Him. May you see motherhood through His eyes, think His thoughts, and treat your child the way He does. When your little flock needs comfort, companionship, or correction, may you turn your eyes toward Jesus, hold His little ones close, and show them the Good Shepherd.*

Chapter 2

GOD'S FULL ATTENTION

*"Man shall not live by bread alone,
but by every word that comes
from the mouth of God."*

—MATTHEW 4:4

EXPECT GOD TO GIVE YOU HIS FULL ATTENTION THROUGH HIS WORD

My dear dad gave me my first alarm clock when I was twelve years old. For the next fifteen years, I woke up to its chipper "beep, beep, beep" and popped out of bed after a good night's sleep. Whenever I wanted to, I woke up to meet with the Lord, study the Bible, and record my prayers in a journal.

I never once hit the snooze button. (I didn't even know how the snooze feature worked!) That is, until I became a mom. Exhausted by our newborn's all-nighters, I hit "snooze" for a couple of days until reality struck: babies *are* alarm clocks and there is *no* snooze button. As you may imagine, my consistent, clearheaded morning devotions changed drastically. Reading the Bible was still important to me—maybe even more so now—but I didn't "pop out" of bed anymore. Instead, I'd wake up to the sound of my daughter's hungry cries and stumble out of bed, straining against the weight of my eyelids and the fog in my brain. One thing was clear: if I wanted to read God's Word during this season of life, I would have to get creative, adjust my expectations, and trust God to feed me while I fed my daughter.

EVEN BETTER THAN COFFEE

Spending time with God in His Word has been an ongoing learning process for me, with one step forward and two steps back, but by His grace, I haven't given up. There's too much at stake. I'm desperate for His friendship. I need His wisdom.

Through the pages of Scripture, Jesus gives us everything we need to do the good work of motherhood. Consider these incredible benefits of God's Word:

- Assures us of God's character in the ups and downs of motherhood.

- Reminds us about our identity in Christ when we feel worthless.

- Helps us discern between things that *sound* right and things that *are* right.

- Upholds Jesus, making Him sweet to us.

- Reveals the ugly underbelly of sin, making it bitter.

- Equips us to do good work.

- Refreshes us when we feel depleted.

- Cheers us on when we want to quit.

- Gives us life-sustaining truths to share with our children.

- Steadies us in the storms of life.

- Gives us hope for the future when today seems so hard.

And that's just the beginning of the Bible's benefits for moms. Can you imagine how you would feel with these blessings to strengthen you from day to day? (Can you imagine how you would feel without them?) The Word of God is precisely what we need to raise our kids in this dark world. God shines the lantern of His Word, helping us navigate a path that is often fraught with unknowns.

If the Word of God is such a precious gift for moms, why do we often feel like it is a burden? Why does it seem so elusive—especially during the early years when sleep is sporadic and our baby needs us around the clock? Especially during the middle years when our days are full of errands, lessons, and playdates? Especially during the teen years when we are up at night, talking with our teen, or waiting for them to come home? Especially during the young-adult phase when we are grappling with our child's adult-sized responsibilities and setbacks? Especially in the grandparent years when our energy flags and our familial demands increase rather than decrease?

These questions are worth our serious consideration. There must be a way for you and me to enjoy the gift of God's Word on a regular basis no matter how busy or exhausted we are. But first, we need to debunk two conflicting messages that moms receive regarding the Bible.

> *Let's not toss God's Word overboard like excess baggage or lug it around like a ball and chain. Instead, let's receive it for what it is: a gift intended to bless us every day.*

The Word of God is luggage on a sinking ship. When we are in the throes of motherhood and we need to streamline our commitments, the Word of God is often the first thing to go. Everything else seems too urgent, but the reality is that we need the Word of God to adequately face those demands. Well-intentioned people pacify mothers by saying, "Don't worry about studying the Bible. It's enough that you are taking care of your child. Give yourself some grace." While I appreciate the effort to lighten our load, these comments aren't helpful. Without God's Word, our burdens increase and motherhood becomes unbearable. The Word of God isn't reserved for well-rested, super-focused, single adults. It's also for exhausted, often-interrupted busy moms. Instead of tossing Scripture off the sinking ship, we must cling to it even more: it will preserve our lives.

The Word of God is a ball and chain. Other well-intentioned people say, "There's no excuse for not studying the Bible. Wake up earlier, stay up later, complete your study guide, and contribute meaningfully during discussion time." For an overextended mom, these comments are a burden, not an inspiration.

In this scenario, the Bible becomes just one more thing that needs our attention in a world where *everything* needs our attention: babies, toddlers, children, and teens must be fed, washed, clothed, held, comforted, inspired, enjoyed, taught, and discipled. Husbands, churches, neighbors, schools, teachers, lessons, sports, and jobs all need our attention. Our own bodies, minds, and emotions need our attention. Then, just when we are about to collapse into bed, we remember that the Bible needs our attention too. No wonder we struggle to get around to it.

But what if we looked at it through God's eyes? He doesn't think the Bible needs our attention. On the contrary, He thinks we need the Bible's attention. God says His Word is like food for the hungry, money for the poor, a light for the traveler, a surgeon for the injured, and a balm for the wounded. The Bible doesn't need us: we need it. Doesn't that just melt your heart? Doesn't it make you stop in your tracks, open your arms, and say, "Yes, Lord. I desperately need Your full attention"?

Let's neither toss God's Word overboard nor lug it around like a ball and chain. Instead, let's receive it for what it is: a gift intended to bless us every day.

RIGHT HANDLING OF THE WORD OF GOD

On my late July walk in the country, I pass by two neighboring gardens. In one, the cornstalks are taller than I am. They are a luscious shade of green and the corn is almost ready to be harvested. In the other, the cornstalks are knee-high. The scraggly leaves are yellowing and turning in on themselves. There will be no harvest. The gardeners used different techniques: one planted the corn in a well-ordered square, watering it faithfully, while the other scattered the corn throughout the garden—one stalk by the carrots, another by the tomatoes—and did not water it. The message is abundantly clear: the way a gardener sows and cultivates her seeds makes all the difference in producing food.

> *If you are new to Bible study, please don't feel intimidated. God intends for the Bible to be accessible to all of us.*

The same principle applies to God's Word. The way we read and respond to God's Word makes all the difference in producing growth. We can hear the importance of the apostle Paul's encouragement to Timothy: "Do your best to present yourself to God as one approved, a worker who has no need to be ashamed, rightly handling the word of truth" (2 Tim. 2:15). Even when we are consuming smaller portions of Scripture and suffering from "mom brain," we can learn how to approach the Bible the way God intends. If you are new to Bible study, please don't feel intimidated. The Bible is accessible to all of us, and we can find lots of support as we connect with friends, teachers, and pastors who honor God's Word and want to help us grow in our Bible literacy.

Over the years, I've learned to ask six basic questions that help me discover what God is communicating through Scripture and how I should respond. Here's a summary of what I've learned. I hope it strengthens you in your Bible reading.

What does it say about God? This is key. Scripture is about God and for God's glory. It is not human-inspired. Humanity is not the central figure or the hero. The Bible reveals everything we need to know about God and compels us to worship the true hero, Jesus.

Why was it written? The author's original intent determines how we read and apply the text. Keep your eye open for who wrote the passage, to whom he was writing, and how the original readers may have received the message. This will help you read the passage in context and discover important things like whether or not a certain message is intended solely for the original reader, for all people, for Christians exclusively, and so on.

What is the genre? The genre, or literary style, of the passage matters and affects the way we interpret it too. Poetry, prophecy, history, parable, and proverb each carries its own implications: recognizing the genre of the passage will help us know how to interpret it correctly.

What does it say?
What does it mean?
What does it mean for me?

Asking these three questions in this order helps us understand the text and know how to apply it. First, we look for what the words literally say (this sounds simple, but it's often overlooked and leads to misinterpretation). Then, we look for what the passage means in its original context (this goes along with the previous question, "Why was it written?"). Finally, we can understand what the passage means for us and how we should respond.

These basic guidelines will keep us from error and help us make the most of our time in God's Word. The garden of our hearts and minds will be lush and productive. The harvest will be sure.

Let's ask God for the wisdom and creativity to draw near to Him through His Word. A verse on an index card by the kitchen sink may be like the cup of water a marathon runner grabs along her race route.

The days of motherhood fly by. Time is of the essence. By God's grace, let's navigate the constantly changing seasons of motherhood and be grateful for any way we can savor God's Word. Instead of wishing for the devotional life we may have had before children, let's discover what a devotional life looks like now: with a baby in our arms, a teen needing a ride, or a grandchild coming over after school. On demanding days, a verse on an index card by the kitchen sink may be like the cup of water a marathon runner grabs along her race route. The Holy Spirit will use that one verse to refuel us. On other days—even most days—we will be capable of more than a moment of prayer or a brief reflection here or there. On those days, let's challenge ourselves to dig in. The Holy Spirit will faithfully use the words on the page to shape our character, prepare us for our day's work, and increase our love for Christ. Rest assured that every bit matters: God promises "my word . . . shall accomplish that which I purpose, and shall succeed in the thing for which I sent it" (Isa. 55:11). Let's ask God for the wisdom and creativity to draw near to Him through His Word.

MOM-FRIENDLY WAYS TO FEAST ON HIS WORD

As we wrap up this chapter, consider these practical, tried-and-true, mom-friendly ways to feast on God's Word. Which one works for you in this season of life?

- Begin with a verse you know. Meditate on it by repeating it thoughtfully, emphasizing a different word each time. For example:

    "**He** *will . . . gently lead those that are with young.*"
    "*He* **will** *. . . gently lead those that are with young.*"
    "*He will . . .* **gently** *lead those that are with young.*"
    "*He will . . . gently* **lead** *those that are with young.*"

- Use a verse to shape your prayers. For example, "*Thank You, Jesus, that You will gently lead me today. Give me grace to follow You.*"

- Ask the Holy Spirit to bring a certain Scripture to mind when you need it most. For example, lately, I rely on Him to remind me, "Serve the Lord with gladness! Come into his presence with singing!" (Ps. 100:2). The Holy Spirit nourishes me with this encouragement as I serve my children.

- Ask a woman who loves God's Word to teach you how to study Scripture or to read through portions of Scripture with you. Be honest about the amount of time and energy you can devote to the study.

- Pursue at least one friendship with a woman who knows and lives by God's Word. Ask her to send you snippets of what she is learning. One of my closest friends often sends a verse to me, taken right out of her own morning devotions. She turns my eyes to Jesus before I launch into a busy day of life-with-littles. It would also be wonderful to be a friend like this for someone else.

need to do this more

- Learn alongside your child. Even though I studied the Bible before motherhood, I never understood the big picture of Scripture until I read *The Jesus Storybook Bible* by Sally Lloyd-Jones with my five-year-old. What a life-changing experience! Keep your heart warm to the Bible verses you are sharing with your child. They are for you too.

- Place an open Bible in a location where you spend a lot of time and read it through the day for nearness to Christ.

- Subscribe to receive a Verse of the Day in a format that you are likely to see, read, and meditate upon.

- Listen to songs with Scripture-based lyrics. I play Seeds Family Worship, Songs for Saplings, and other Scripture songs for my children, and the Lord uses them to nourish me too.

- <u>Write</u> a verse on an index card and read it through the day.
- Choose Scripture-rich artwork for your home. Get in the habit of pausing to read it and take it in. Point it out to your child and read it together often.
- Get in a good, solid church. If you miss the pastor's sermon on Sunday, listen to an audio recording during the week or watch the service online if that's an option. This will benefit you in two ways: you'll be nourished by the Word, and you'll stay connected with your church family.
- Whenever a season of motherhood allows, *do* join a Bible study with other people.
- Whenever a season of motherhood allows, *do* wake up early to read God's Word and pray.
- Whenever a season of motherhood demands everything you've got, *do* remember this:

For I am convinced that neither death nor life, neither angels nor demons, neither the present nor the future, nor any powers, neither height nor depth, nor anything else in all creation, will be able to separate us from the love of God that is in Christ Jesus our Lord.—Romans 8:38–39 NIV

RECEIVING GOD'S FULL ATTENTION

Something to cherish:

For the word of God is living and active, sharper than any two-edged sword, piercing to the division of soul and of spirit, of joints and of marrow, and discerning the thoughts and intentions of the heart. —Hebrews 4:12

Something to sing:

"Fighting Words" by Ellie Holcomb

Something to read:

Women of the Word: How to Study the Bible with Both Our Hearts and Our Minds by Jen Wilkin

Something to consider:

- Do I cherish God's Word? If not, can I ask God to help me to cherish it? *Ask for more desire to learn it*

- How can I get creative, adjust expectations, or learn to trust God when it comes to reading the Bible? What are one or two practices I can begin now to prioritize God's Word? *Read for 5 mins wry night?*

- Who can I involve in this new practice (child, friend, spouse, younger/older woman)? *Husband C. 10 mins w/the kids?*

MY PRAYER FOR YOU: *May you receive the caring attention of God's Word as it fills your thoughts, shapes your words, and informs your choices. May God give you the blessing of a local church where the Bible is taught faithfully. May you grow to love the Word of God and have at least one good friend who loves it too.*

Chapter 3

AN EARNEST PRAYER LIFE

What I know not, teach me.
What I am not, make me.
What I have not, give me.

—OLD ANGLICAN PRAYER

EXPECT GOD TO LISTEN TO YOU WHEN YOU PRAY

If you flipped through my journals from our first few years of marriage, you'd come across a prayer I wrote when we stopped using birth control and asked God for a baby. It's a sweet prayer, naively believing that because Ryan and I were ready to have a baby, God would give us a baby. We had purchased our first home and were excited to start our family (whether that meant six kids or two). For the first few months, we were bright-eyed and confident: *it will happen any day now.* Then, week after week and month after month, the negative pregnancy tests piled up. I began to worry. *Perhaps something is wrong. Perhaps I can't get pregnant.*

With every negative pregnancy test, our desire for a child grew. Every week at our small group meeting we would share the same prayer request: "Please ask God to give us a baby." We rarely asked for prayer about anything else: all other needs paled in comparison. We longed for a baby. As the months rolled by with more negative tests, we exhausted our family and friends with our persistent request. "Please ask God to give us a baby."

THE GIFT OF PRAYER

Eventually, my doctor diagnosed me with PCOS, which at that time in medical history basically meant, we don't know why you aren't getting pregnant.

Research suggested that if I removed carbohydrates from my diet, my body might go into ketosis and jump-start the ovulation process. I tried it. For the next year, I meticulously avoided all carbs; even a crumb would threaten this fragile experiment with my broken body. As you can imagine, I was constantly hungry. I remember saying, "I wouldn't do this for any other reason than to have a baby, but I will do it forever if it means I have a chance."

My expectations for an easy-peasy motherhood had come to

a screeching halt. Suddenly, everything felt impossible—and out of my control. It reminded me of the futile attempt to make a fire with two sticks: you try and try and try without a hint of a spark. You may be freezing, starving, and you must have a fire or perish, but no sparks fly. That's what infertility felt like to me. No matter how desperately I wanted a baby, or how diligently I worked, or how often we tried, or how many doctors we saw, or how long I stared at each pregnancy test willing it to produce a second pink line, I could not make a baby.

When I prayed, I didn't receive reliable confirmation that God would give me a baby, but through Scripture, I did receive confirmation that He was listening and He cared.

Every day, I woke up early in the morning and met with God in prayer. I poured out my heart and extended my empty hands. I often thought of Hannah in the Bible. She, too, was desperate for a baby, "deeply distressed and prayed to the LORD and wept bitterly" (1 Sam. 1:10). She, too, was hungry in body and soul. She went to the temple to beseech the Lord for a son and vowed she would "give him to the LORD all the days of his life" (v. 11). The Bible says she was praying in such a way that Eli, the priest, reprimanded her for being drunk. She replied,

> "No, my lord, I am a woman troubled in spirit. I have drunk neither wine nor strong drink, but I have been pouring out my soul before the LORD. Do not regard your servant as a

worthless woman, for all along I have been speaking out of
my great anxiety and vexation." (vv. 15–16)

I could relate. I, too, knew what it was like to pour out my soul before the Lord. I, too, knew Him to be a refuge, protecting me from the embarrassment of an onlooker's judgment. Oh, how I desperately wished I could relate to Hannah's entire story—and to hear Eli's comforting reply, "Go in peace, and the God of Israel grant your petition that you have made to him" (v. 17). Hannah got up and ate. "Her face was no longer sad" and she worshiped the Lord (vv. 18–19). Shortly thereafter, she conceived and gave birth to a son.

When I prayed, I didn't receive reliable confirmation that God would give me a baby. But through Scripture, I did receive confirmation that He was listening and He cared. Although God was not filling my womb, He was teaching me how to pray from a mother-like heart: first, to acknowledge that maternal love is wildly beyond my control, and second, to boldly present my requests while humbly surrendering to His sovereign will.

I know exactly what Ellen Cantarow meant when she wrote, "Making the decision to have a child—it's momentous. It is to decide forever to have your heart go walking around outside your body."[3] What joy. What agony. What helplessness. For better or worse, motherhood intensifies our emotions and challenges our thought-lives like nothing else can. Our response to this beautiful upheaval really matters. If left to our own devices, we'd quickly become self-focused, child-focused, controlling, anxious, angry, cynical, or numb. We'd either vent or stuff our emotions, never finding lasting relief. But if, through prayer, we share our thoughts and emotions with God, we will find a faithful friend who both listens and speaks the truth in love. After all, when you feel like your heart is walking around outside your body, you need supernatural help. You need wisdom, comfort, and power. God knows this. That's why He gives us the gift of prayer.

Prayer connects us with God and grounds us in His truth. Through His atoning death on the cross, Jesus welcomes us into God's presence no matter how we are feeling: whether we are devastated, anxious, coldhearted, discontent, raving mad, illogical, weary, jubilant . . . or serene. Jesus understands. He sympathizes with our weaknesses. He invites us to "draw near to the throne of grace, that we may receive mercy and find grace to help in time of need." And even to draw close "with confidence" (Heb. 4:16).

We can pray about anything. God wants to hear from us day or night about whatever is on our minds. No lament is too raw. No request is too extravagant. No murmur is too humble for His ear. God listens to every word. Then He speaks to us through His Word. Prayer and Scripture go hand in hand.

We can also pray the words of Scripture, soaking in them, wrestling with them, and surrendering to them. In the preface to my dog-eared copy of *The One Year Praying through the Bible for Your Kids,* author Nancy Guthrie humbly confesses,

> Over the years, my prayers have tended to be more
> self-directed than Scripture-saturated, which means that I

pray the same thing over and over. My prayers have often been shaped more by my stunted and sometimes selfish desires for my child than by God's grand purposes for all of his children. So I need the Scriptures to inform and direct my prayers and to encourage me to persevere in prayer. I need the Word of God to provide me with fresh words and renewed passion to pray for my child day by day.[4]

I love this. When my desires as a mom are amiss, Scripture will straighten them out. When my understanding is limited, Scripture will direct me to the truth. When my soul is immature or apathetic, Scripture will lift my eyes, increase my appetite, and exercise my ability to care. As I run to God's throne on behalf of my children, I want all of this. Don't you?

EARNEST PRAYER IS EFFECTIVE

Scripture is clear: God answers our prayers and often grants our requests. Children are born, healed, helped, and saved because mothers pray for them. Mothers, too, receive what they need—from endurance to practical assistance—because they ask God for it. Scripture compels us to persist in prayer: in some unfathomable way, we move God's heart and provoke Him to action (Luke 18:1–8). Think of Hannah who prayed persistently for a son, and then, with baby Samuel in her arms said, "For this child I prayed, and the LORD has granted me my petition that I made to him" (1 Sam.1:27). Think of James who wrote,

The prayer of a righteous person has great power as it is working. Elijah was a man with a nature like ours, and he prayed fervently that it might not rain, and for three years and six months it did not rain on the earth. Then he prayed again, and heaven gave rain, and the earth bore its fruit.
—James 5:16–18

Think of Jesus who, while on earth, prayed often and, now in heaven, continues to pray for His beloved flock (see Heb. 7:25; Rom. 8:34). Think of Scripture's countless examples of people who spoke to God *and He responded.*

Contrary to popular belief, God does not just respond to prayer with yes, no, or wait. He is a divine person who responds to us as a person would: with questions, stories, compassion, silence, song, predictability, and surprise. God wants us to tell Him what we need, and He wants to answer us in an ongoing conversation. Perhaps God wants us to pray so we see our dependence on Him. Perhaps He wants us to pray so we are prepared to receive our request or to become the change agent for the very thing we want (1 Thess. 5:17). Or perhaps He simply wants to be our dearest friend. I don't know why prayer is so important to God, but I know that it

> *He will not grant our requests when He plans to give us something far greater than we can imagine. If every Little League season went according to a mom's prayers, there would be plenty of grand slams, but not much character development.*

is, and I know that God will move heaven and earth to respond to us according to His perfect will (see John 14:13–14; 16:23–24; 1 John 5:14–15).

So, I'm going for it. By God's grace, I'm going to be a praying mom. Want to join me? We can pray expectantly for every aspect of our children's lives. We can pray for our child's:

- Salvation and joy in Christ
- Wholehearted love of God and people
- Physical, emotional, mental, and spiritual well-being
- Character, obedience to Christ, and light in the world
- Friends, family, and local church
- Rest, work, and pleasure
- Past, including forgiveness and healing
- Present, including grace and faithfulness
- Future, including wisdom and endurance

Our prayers will directly impact our children. God will grant our requests—sometimes before the words even leave our mouths and other times after years of waiting. We will be amazed by the beautiful union of our ordinary prayers and our Maker's compassionate heart.

WHEN GOD DOESN'T GRANT OUR REQUESTS

Our desires don't always align with God's will to exalt Jesus and establish His kingdom. He will not grant our requests when He plans to give us something far greater than we can imagine (Eph. 3:20–21). If every Little League season went according to a mom's prayers, there would be plenty of grand slams, but not much character development. From our innocuous prayers about home runs and science quizzes to serious petitions about mental health and future spouses, we pray through a limited lens. If we could see into the future and comprehend the scope of history, we would want God's will—and not our own will—every time.

Jesus taught us to pray, "Your kingdom come, your will be done, on earth as it is in heaven" (Matt. 6:10). As He approached the moment when He would bear God's wrath and judgment for all humanity, Jesus showed us what it looks like to surrender to God's sovereign will. On the night before His crucifixion, Jesus was "very sorrowful, even to death" (Matt. 26:38). He

> *God works through motherhood to teach us how to share our thoughts and feelings with Him, to ask Him to provide for our needs, and to trust Him even when our will differs from His.*

struggled through prayer, pleading, "My Father, if it be possible, let this cup pass from me; nevertheless, not as I will, but as you will" (v. 39). Blessedly, Jesus "endured the cross, despising the shame" because He knew God would only require His death on a cross if it led to our redemption (Heb. 12:2). When we pray, we, too, must ultimately surrender to God's will.

It is not easy to surrender. When God's will does not make sense to me—and when it tastes bitter—I return to Hannah's second prayer to learn from a mom who surrendered to God time and time again. She begins by praising God for His sovereignty. She continues,

> *"There is none holy like the LORD:*
> *for there is none besides you;*
> *there is no rock like our God.*
> *Talk no more so very proudly,*
> *let not arrogance come from your mouth;*
> *for the LORD is a God of knowledge,*
> *and by him actions are weighed."*—1 Samuel 2:2–3

Hannah is a faithful mentor to us, passing along truths to help us make sense of motherhood. She wants us to see that God rules over all the earth. He is exalted and there is no one like Him. He declares "the end from the beginning and from ancient times things not yet done, saying, 'My counsel shall stand, and I will accomplish all my purpose'" (Isa. 46:10). Our lives will go according to His plan. Period. As Hannah suggests, we must put our hands over our mouths and kneel in surrender.

This is a severe mercy, and every wise mother embraces it with all her heart. Yet, as Hannah found, we can affirm that God also responds to—and often grants—our petitions. The psalmist says, "He fulfills the desire of those who fear him; he also hears their cry and saves them" (Ps. 145:19). When we approach the throne of grace through prayer, we behold the mysterious union of God's immutable will and His kind, responsive ear.

• • •

One day, weary from months and months of infertility, I came across this quote from St. Therese of Lisieux: "God gives me whatever I want, because I want whatever He gives." The agony of longing for a child and the awe of surrendering to God swept over me. St. Therese must have wrestled, struggled, and suffered through a lifetime of prayer to arrive at such serenity and trust. May you and I arrive there too.

RECEIVING AN EARNEST PRAYER LIFE

Something to cherish:

Since then we have a great high priest who has passed through the heavens, Jesus, the Son of God, let us hold fast our confession. For we do not have a high priest who is unable to sympathize with our weaknesses, but one who in every respect has been tempted as we are, yet without sin. Let us then with confidence draw near to the throne of grace, that we may receive mercy and find grace to help in time of need. —Hebrews 4:14–16

Something to sing:

"Never Would've Made It" by Unspoken

Something to read:

The One Year Praying through the Bible for Your Kids by Nancy Guthrie

Something to consider:

- What is my prayer life like? What do I wish it were like?

- Heavenly Father, what is on Your heart for my child today?

- These are the motherhood needs I want to pray about today:

  Physical:
  Emotional:
  Spiritual:
  Intellectual:
  Relational:

MY PRAYER FOR YOU: *May you know that you are never alone. Our great God sees you, loves you, and knows you by name. He wants to hear from you. May you have faith to pour your heart out in prayer.*

Chapter 4

IRONCLAD TRUST IN GOD'S PROMISES

*And this is the promise
that he made to us—eternal life.*

—1 JOHN 2:25

EXPECT TO BE DEVASTATED BY SIN AND COMFORTED BY GOD'S MERCY

During our long months of infertility, I took too many pregnancy tests.[5] When I discovered tests at the dollar store, I bought them in bulk and used them whenever the unknown felt unbearable, which was often. Each test gave me three minutes to believe that, maybe this time, God had granted my request for a baby. I knew better than to stare at the test as the three minutes ticked by, but

I couldn't help myself. A pink streak would move across the test strip, giving me momentary hope as it seemed to slow down and almost mark the positive line before gliding by, leaving a single pink control line. My hopes faded as the rest of the test strip turned maddeningly white. I'd tilt my head and squint my eyes for any sign of a second line, but these $1.00 tests were brutally honest: negative again.

The instruction pamphlet clearly stated that the results would be invalid after three minutes and the test should be discarded immediately. Nonetheless, I'd tuck each negative test in the medicine cabinet and look at it through the day because sometimes after an hour or two, a ghost line would appear. The test would look positive because the ink had bled through and made a second line. In my heart, I knew the result was invalid, but each ghost line gave me a reason to take another test. Sometimes, I'd take multiple tests in a row just in case my body needed the extra five minutes to develop enough pregnancy hormones to turn the next test positive. Whenever the result was negative—and they all were for over a year—I was crushed. My only reprieve from the grief of infertility was in those three minutes of possibility.

THE UNSINKABLE ARK

Every time I took a pregnancy test, I thought about Noah on the ark, surrounded by a world of water, sending out birds to look for evidence of dry land, hoping that someday he and his family would build a home and plow a field on solid ground. I imagined Noah launching each raven or dove with a prayer: "Is it *now,* Lord? Is this the time we exit the ark?" Scripture does not condemn Noah for releasing birds in expectation of dry land. On the contrary, Noah's faith was credited to him as righteousness (Heb. 11:7). Although he didn't know the specific details of God's plan—like when the ark would land or when his family would exit the ark—he knew it would land. God had promised. Noah built the ark and climbed aboard with ironclad trust in God's promise to save him and his family.

You and I share something in common with Noah: the circumstances of our lives are mysterious—known only to God and revealed to us in the moment—but God's promises are clear, made known to us through Scripture. We can count on them. They are our unsinkable ark.

God never promised me a baby the way He promised Noah dry ground. I wish He had. I wish I could have counted on it. Nonetheless, I knew I could count on His love for me, and I knew He would answer my supplication if it was His will. I'd take each pregnancy test and wonder, "Is it *now,* Lord? Is this the time you will give us a baby?" I had so much riding on God's decision—my hopes and dreams for a baby, yes, but also my career, ministry work, and aspirations for higher education. I wanted to know how I should plan for the future, but I was quickly learning that uncertainty is par for the course in motherhood as in life.

God allowed me to endure the tumultuous waters of infertility for reasons beyond my comprehension. I do know one thing:

> *Through infertility,
> I learned that I
> could trust God
> to wrap His arms
> around me when
> mine were empty.
> He taught me that
> I need His promises
> more than I need
> a baby.*

He worked through infertility to correct my trust problem. I had been trusting in motherhood, hoping that a baby would stabilize and satisfy me. By withholding this blessing, God was inviting me to trust in Him alone. He was teaching me that some things, like husbands, children, health, and careers, are not promised to me, while other things—like God's steadfast love, faithfulness, and forgiveness—are. I learned that I don't need what is not promised (no matter how much I may want it), but I do need what is promised.

Through infertility, God taught me that I need His promises more than I need a baby. After all, a baby cannot assure me of my worth or satisfy my soul, but Jesus can—and will. With every negative pregnancy test, I learned to lift my eyes from my frustrating body and set my sights on heaven, where my physical body will be restored and death will be no more. I learned that God loves and enjoys me; He has good work for me to do with or without a baby. Most of all, I learned that I could trust God to wrap His arms around me even when mine were empty.

We all place our trust in something: if not in God, then in our child, career, friends, money, personal strengths, or even a personal vice. The challenges of motherhood expose every false sense of security and point us to our only source of stability: the unshakeable promises of God.

One of my favorite examples of a woman who developed ironclad trust in God's promises is Mary, the mother of Jesus. Mary navigated uncertainty through a lens that kept her upright and secure. She was the first woman to experience motherhood on this side of redemptive history. Jesus was both her child and her Savior. Every aspect of Mary's motherhood was connected to Jesus' incarnation: Jesus arrived in her womb as a miraculous gift from the Holy Spirit and He was with her as she went through pregnancy, delivered a baby, raised a teenager, sent her adult child off into the world, and then—with unspeakable sorrow—watched Him be crucified and buried. He was with her when she worshiped Him as her resurrected Lord.

Through Mary's life, we hear Jesus say to mothers, *I am right here for you. I have always been right here for you.* Mary shows us why—and how—to trust God's promises as we raise our children. I want us to look closely at Mary's first experiences as a mom and consider three things we can do to exercise trust in God's promises: we can take comfort in the covenant of grace, call to mind God's acts of deliverance, and rest on His strength.[6]

EXERCISE TRUST IN GOD'S PROMISES

Take Comfort in the Covenant of Grace

Mary's faith in God is grounded in God's covenant of grace. He promised to be the God of His people and to establish an everlasting kingdom. He promised that one of their offspring—the

Messiah—would crush the head of the adversary. Over time, God revealed His covenant with increasing clarity to Adam and Eve, Noah, Abraham, Moses, David, and the prophets. For thousands of years, Mary's ancestors wrestled with God's covenant of grace. Sometimes, they believed; sometimes, they doubted. But it marked them in every way as they circumcised their sons, celebrated feasts, and kept the Levitical law. They wrote, sang, and prayed about God's covenant of grace, asking repeatedly, "Is it *now,* Lord? Is this the time You will send the Messiah?"

Mary herself, perhaps weary of waiting, may have lifted her eyes to heaven and asked, "Is it *now,* Lord?" Then one day, in the sixth month of the days of Herod, God sent Gabriel to Nazareth to say yes. The time had come. The Messiah was on His way.

In the biblical account, Gabriel appears to Mary and says, "Greetings, O favored one, the Lord is with you." Mary trembles in fear, but Gabriel comforts her saying, "Do not be afraid, Mary, for you have found favor with God." He goes on to tell her that she will bear a baby boy, the "Son of the Most High" (see Luke 1:28–33).

Mary's reply? "Behold, I am the servant of the Lord; let it be to me according to your word" (v. 38).

When Gabriel revealed Mary's pregnancy to her, it was about so much more than baby bottles and onesies: it was about the long-awaited Messiah finally coming to save His people. Though she trembled in fear, Mary took comfort in this: God was keeping His covenant of grace.

You and I can be comforted by God's covenant of grace too. When faced with the uncertainties of motherhood, we can count on Jesus, who demonstrated just how far God would go to keep His promises. Though sin seeps into every aspect of motherhood, we know we have peace with God through Christ. Though our bodies and minds fail us, we know we have hope in God who will redeem all things (Rom. 5:1–5). Recently, our pastor comforted our congregation with these words; "If you are a believer in Jesus, you are an heir of the covenant of grace. God promises to be God to you and to your children forever." God kept His covenant of grace: He gave us Jesus. This is comforting indeed.

Call to Mind God's Acts of Deliverance

Soon after hearing from Gabriel, Mary visits her cousin Elizabeth, who celebrates Mary's burgeoning trust in God, proclaiming, "Blessed is she who believed that there would be a fulfillment of what was spoken to her from the Lord" (see Luke 1:42–45). Right then and there, Mary sings a song calling to mind God's mighty acts of deliverance. For centuries, people all over the world have recited, prayed, and sung this new mom's song of ironclad trust in her Savior. We call it "The Magnificat." I invite you to read it in your Bible, in Luke 1:46–55.

If Mary had looked only to her present circumstances, she would have collapsed in fear, but she looks at God and remembers His acts of deliverance. Mary sees herself on a timeline of people—some proud and mighty, others humble and hungry—all in God's sovereign hand. She thinks about the generations of people who have been waiting for the Messiah to come and about the future generations who will be blessed by His coming.

She sees herself in the context of history, from God's covenant with Abraham into the future where you and I sit, needing God's salvation in the twenty-first century.

When you and I are faced with uncertainty in motherhood, we, too, can remember God's acts of deliverance. We are not Mary, but we, too, are on the timeline of history—preceded by billions of people and, perhaps, preceding billions more; people in all manner of circumstances, cultures, customs, and languages— under God's watchful eye, in His powerful hand, and part of the story of redemption. Can you see yourself there, holding your child in your arms? Can you see God there, too, thoroughly invested in *your* moment, clothed in majesty, kindness, and power for you? Your place in history emanates with the presence of Jesus, the long-awaited Messiah. He who bound Himself to His people thousands of years ago has kept His promise. Oh, that you and I would develop Mary's God-centered mindset as we travel this road with our dear children!

Rest on the Strength of the Deliverer

Soon after the birth of Jesus, Mary receives some unlikely visitors: shepherds arrive at the stable. While they were watching their sheep at night, the glory of the Lord shone around them and the angel of the Lord appeared to them, told them not to be afraid, and announced the "good news of great joy that will be for all the people. For unto you is born this day in the city of David a Savior, who is Christ the Lord" (Luke 2:10–11).

Tradition tells us that these shepherds may have tended the

sheep that birthed the lambs used as sin sacrifices at the temple. When a lamb was born without blemish, it was wrapped in cloths and laid in a manger so it would not become injured or marred. If this is accurate, these shepherds would have understood what the angels were saying: Jesus was the perfect Lamb of God—wrapped in swaddling cloths and lying in the manger—come to pay the penalty for their sin. They left everything to find Him.

I can relate to the shepherds. I, too, need the Lamb of God to take away my sin. One of the hardest parts of motherhood is seeing the extent of my own sinful heart. I hate the way I sometimes resent, manipulate, idolize, stifle, neglect, judge, envy, mislead, and belittle my children. And yet, the glory of the Lord shines around me with good news: a spotless Lamb has come to take away my sin. Jesus covers the most bitter part of motherhood—my sin—with the sweetest part: Himself, my Savior.

I hate the way I sometimes resent, manipulate, mislead, and belittle my children. And yet, the glory of the Lord shines around me with good news: a spotless Lamb has been born to take away my sin.

There sits Mary, a new mother, facing a world of unknowns, yet trusting God to do everything He said He would do. She treasures the shepherds' message and ponders it in her heart. She doesn't take matters into her own hands or badger God about when and how it will happen; she simply believes the promise and rests in her strong Deliverer.

You and I can rest in Him too, knowing how much He cares about our uncertainty in motherhood. He hears our cries and knows our longings. He forgives our sin and delivers us from evil. And, one day soon, He will return from heaven and shine love's pure light. He promised.

• • •

One autumn morning seventeen years ago, I woke up and took a pregnancy test. I tore open the packaging, took the test, saw the negative results, and, this time, tossed it in the trash can. When I got out of the shower, I glanced at the rejected test. I blinked and looked again.

I saw two pink lines.

I picked up the test and looked at it more closely.

I had only been in the shower for five minutes.

It was possible.

I didn't know what to do with myself. On my way to work, I stopped by the doctor's office for a blood test to confirm the pregnancy. The doctor prepared me for the worst. "You know, you're not supposed to read pregnancy tests after three minutes. It's probably a false positive."

"I know," I said, meaning it. "I know."

She told me to call for the results in the afternoon. I had been going through the motions of teaching poetry and grading papers, but all I could think about was the possibility that I was pregnant. After work, I called the doctor's office. I held my breath as I waited to connect with a nurse. I will never forget her response.

She looked at the results of the blood test and said, "Well, it's very early, but you are pregnant."

After all those agonizing months of waiting, you'd think I would have screamed, or jumped up and down, or bubbled over in excitement, but I didn't. I just exhaled. Later, when I saw Ryan, I blurted out, "I'm pregnant." We laughed, cried, and held each other, amazed.

We estimated that our baby was the size of the period at the end of this sentence and yet we were already in love with her. God had granted our relentless requests. We bowed under the holiness of it all and thanked Him. Then we went to the store and bought the coziest baby blanket on the planet.

God's promises stood firm on that happy day, and on all other days, before and since.

RECEIVING IRONCLAD TRUST IN GOD'S PROMISES

Something to cherish:

For all the promises of God find their Yes in him. That is why it is through him that we utter our Amen to God for his glory. And it is God who establishes us with you in Christ, and has anointed us, and who has also put his seal on us and given us his Spirit in our hearts as a guarantee.
—2 Corinthians 1:20–22

Something to sing:

"Oh! Great Is Our God!" by Brian Eichelberger, The Sing Team

Something to read:

Devoted: Great Men and Their Godly Moms by Tim Challies

Something to consider:

- What detail about Mary's perspective do I want to remember?

- What part of motherhood do I need to surrender to the Lord and remember His acts of deliverance and His promises?

- How has God delivered me in the past?

- How do God's promises shape the way I see my circumstances today? How will they shape the way I raise my child?

- How will I intentionally pursue a mindset like Mary's and remember God's promises from day to day?

Chapter 5

SELFLESSNESS THAT PRODUCES FRUIT

Plough deep in me, great Lord,
heavenly husbandman,
That my being may be a tilled field,
The roots of grace spreading far and wide,
Until thou alone art seen in me,
Thy beauty golden like summer harvest,
Thy fruitfulness as autumn plenty.
—THE VALLEY OF VISION[7]

EXPECT JESUS TO GROW
SOMETHING BEAUTIFUL IN YOU

As I was straightening my classroom at the end of a busy school day, a smile crossed my face as I remembered my students' rousing discussion about Shakespeare's *Hamlet*. I also smiled because I was pregnant. (Finally!) At thirty-one weeks, my baby bump was approaching basketball size and I was counting down the days until I would meet our baby girl face-to-face.

I thought about her constantly and filled my journal with prayers for her. My students offered baby name suggestions—some adorable, some bizarre, and a few, when combined with my unique last name, downright hilarious. I had never been happier. I was arranging a small stack of books on a shelf when, suddenly, I felt an intense pain unlike anything I had ever felt before. I stopped and caught my breath. A few minutes later, I felt the pain again. *Was I in labor?* A pang of fear and a thrill of excitement rushed over me at the same time. I gathered my things and headed home.

Ryan and I went to the doctor's office as soon as possible. After a thorough ultrasound, the doctor told me I was 90 percent effaced and beginning to dilate. I was in preterm labor and we had to take immediate action. Moments later, I was wheeled into an ambulance and barreled fifty miles down the highway to a hospital with a specialized NICU department.

FOREVER CHANGED

To stop contractions and administer a steroid for the baby's lung development, the doctors put me on a three-day treatment of magnesium. It was torturous. I felt like I was burning from the inside out. I begged for relief. Knowing better than I about our perilous condition, the doctor soberly ignored my pleas and increased the dosage. Desperate to help, Ryan spooned ice chips into my mouth and asked family, friends, and church members to pray. The same people who had faithfully asked God to give us this baby returned to their knees and lifted us up to God once again.

After three days, my contractions still persisted, and the doctors braced for a premature delivery. At least the baby had received a full dose of steroids. They allowed me to shower for the first time in days and return to bed. And then, suddenly, without any fanfare, the contractions stopped. Perplexed by this unexpected turn of events, the doctors consulted one another and eventually sent me home on bed rest. We thanked God and sent the good news out to our prayer warriors.

I lay on the couch for a month, passing the time with visitors, good books, and inspiring movies. At week thirty-five, contractions began again. This time, my doctor decided to stop my labor by giving me a light sedative and sending me home to get some sleep. Several hours later, when the contractions hadn't stopped and I hadn't fallen asleep, she knew it was time. I labored intensely for three days and then gave birth to a beautiful baby girl. I was forever changed.

• • •

While early pregnancy had its share of nausea and discomfort, I didn't begin to glimpse the cost of motherhood until that scary evening when I was wheeled out of the hospital on a gurney and into an ambulance headed for the nearest hospital with a

NICU. The slam of the ambulance door still echoes in my mind. It was the first time I had to lay down my life for another person and do whatever it took to protect the baby inside my womb. At the time, it didn't seem like I had much of a choice, but I wouldn't want it any other way. Ready or not, I was beginning to learn an important motherhood lesson: selflessness.

I'm reminded of a conversation I heard between Malcolm Gladwell and Oprah Winfrey.[8] Malcolm Gladwell is a journalist, podcaster, and *New York Times* bestselling author. He travels around the world, interviewing people from all walks of life and wrestling with the complexities of human psychology. You probably know Oprah's vast scope of experiences, conversations, and relationships; it's important to keep this in mind as you read their exchange.

Oprah: What's the most selfless thing you've ever seen? The most selfless thing you've ever witnessed firsthand?

Gladwell: Wow. "Most" is a kind of . . . part of me is like whenever I talk to anyone I know who is a young mother and I figure out how many hours they sleep, you know, is there anything more selfless than that?

Oprah, interjecting: There isn't.

Gladwell: There isn't. So maybe that's it.

Oprah: Nor more selfless than actually being a good mother or a good parent. That would be top of my list. When you think of all of the things that people have to do . . .

go home, you step in the door, there are five kids who don't care that you had a whole day and what happened in that day but you have to be just as you need to be for them in that moment. I don't know anything more selfless than that.

"I DON'T KNOW ANYTHING MORE SELFLESS THAN THAT."

Oprah and Gladwell have seen selfless people in all manner of circumstances. They've talked with Nobel Peace Prize winners, civil rights activists, politicians, scientists, artists. And yet, in their eyes, mothers shine the brightest. Even though you and I aren't necessarily looking for Oprah's or Gladwell's approval, isn't it good to be reminded that the sacrifices you make for your child aren't invisible? Your work as a mom impacts civilization because selflessness is the greatest form of love. Jesus said it best when He said, "Greater love has no one than this, that someone lay down his life for his friends" (John 15:13).

Every day, you and I are invited—rather, plunged—into a calling to lay down our lives for our children.

Some women begin learning maternal selflessness long before they have children. Maybe you did. Maybe you were the little girl who practiced motherhood by caring for your baby doll. Maybe you were the teen girl who took the time to eat well, exercise, and sleep soundly not only for her own well-being, but also for her future child's well-being. Maybe you were the young woman who considered her future children when making decisions about college, career, and relationships. Maybe you were the grown woman who learned selflessness as you grappled with a surprise pregnancy, endured a difficult labor, struggled with infertility, welcomed a foster child into your home, or traveled across the world to bring your adopted son or daughter home. Or maybe, like me, you are learning selflessness *today* as you seek the grace to "do nothing from selfish ambition or conceit, but in humility count others more significant than yourselves" (Phil. 2:3).

Every day, you and I are invited—rather, *plunged*—into a calling to lay down our lives for our children; sometimes the pull is so strong it barely feels optional. Selflessness is one of God's gifts to moms. It doesn't always feel like a gift, but if you think about it, mothers change the world with their love, and that's profoundly good.

But is that all there is to motherhood?

Is selflessness the epitome of it all?

Is selflessness the endgame?

I don't think it is.

SELFLESSNESS LEADS TO ABUNDANT LIFE

Let's listen in on something Jesus shared with His disciples shortly before His death. He was explaining why He was about to die and He was urging His disciples—including you and me—to follow His example. Jesus said,

"Truly, truly, I say to you, unless a grain of wheat falls into the earth and dies, it remains alone; but if it dies, it bears much fruit. Whoever loves his life loses it, and whoever hates his life in this world will keep it for eternal life. If anyone serves me, he must follow me; and where I am, there will my servant be also."—John 12:24–26

Here, Jesus is reaching out to people who want everything He has to offer: people like you and me who want to love God, be remade in His image, do good works for His kingdom, and love people for His sake, and He's saying, *The only way for you to truly live is through My death. If you want to bear good fruit, do as I do and lay down your life.*

Soon after, Jesus died and was buried in the ground like a grain of wheat. Then, God raised Him from the grave and He sprang forth with abundant life. That He would "bear much fruit" is the understatement of the ages. By laying down His life, Jesus produced a staggering amount of fruit, and Scripture is replete with what He has done. See Colossians 2:13–15, Luke 4:18, and Matthew 28:18–20 for just a glimpse. Jesus makes one thing abundantly clear: selflessness is not the endgame. It's the beginning of something glorious.

When a grain of wheat is buried in the soil, nutrients feed it until it grows and swells. Its skin stretches, puckers, and cracks open. Roots venture into the soil, searching for water and nutrients. A stem sprouts, tender and thin at first, but soon large enough to push through the soil and unfurl in the sunshine. It grows a sturdy stalk and long leaves. In time, it flowers and goes to seed—and each seed carries the hope of multiplied life.

This simile of what it takes for a grain of wheat to bear fruit helps us to understand what Jesus has done to secure our eternal life and, consequently, what happens in us as we walk with Him through motherhood. First, we place all our hope in Jesus who died and rose again for us.

Then, we lay down our lives, dying to self for our children. We truly suffer, keenly feeling each loss, but Jesus employs every hour of lost sleep, every ounce of physical wear and tear, every emotional up and down, and every act of service to blessedly rid us of ourselves and make us more like Him. He tends us like a garden, causing us to bear good fruit like love, joy, peace, patience, kindness, goodness, faithfulness, gentleness, and self-control. Under His care, we become wholehearted, generous, and brave. Life begins to make sense. Our presence at home and abroad suggests His presence there too. Who could possibly produce this much growth from one surrendered seed—from you, from me? God alone.

PRESS ON WHEN GROWTH SEEMS SLOW

I'm learning not to get discouraged when my spiritual growth seems unremarkable and slow. God works in the circumstances of everyday life and He takes as much time as necessary to cultivate us. We're precious to Him and He treats us carefully. Consider John Owen's explanation of the Christian's growth over time.

The growth of trees and plants takes place so slowly that it is not easily seen. Daily we notice little change. But, in the course of time, we see that a great change has taken place. So it is with grace. Sanctification is a progressive, lifelong work (Prov. 4:18). It is an amazing work of God's grace, and it is a work to be prayed for (Rom. 8:27).[9]

We don't have to hurry, force, or fake the Spirit's fruit; it will grow in time from the inside out as we enjoy our friendship with God. Jesus calls it "abiding" in Him. He says, "I am the vine; you are the branches. Whoever abides in me and I in him, he it is that bears much fruit, for apart from me you can do nothing" (John 15:5).

As we abide in Christ, He makes His fruit grow in us. We see it when, by His grace, we choose to do the right thing, say the life-giving thing, or think the true thing. We see it when we mess up and ask God for mercy, when our desperation causes us to fly to Him for help, and when we begin to cherish the daily suffering of sanctification because it draws us closer to Jesus Himself.

Cling to God in motherhood and you will not come up empty-handed.

Cling to God in motherhood and you will not come up empty-handed. Look for His presence in the deep, dark soil of selflessness and you will find Him cultivating your soul to be like His.

Motherhood isn't just about selflessness.

It's about growth, good fruit, and the glory of God.

REJOICE IN THE GOOD FRUIT
GOD IS PRODUCING IN YOU

Sometimes I overlook the fruit God produces through motherhood because I'm too busy resenting the natural effects of life with kids. All I see is an overflowing diaper bag. Missed deadlines. Crumby floors. Half-finished conversations. Messy hair and tired eyes. I long for the way things were before I had children.

Pining for the old days makes me wish I could get my act together and minimize the ever-burgeoning effect of motherhood. Yes, I want to be a mom, but I also want my pre-mom lifestyle (especially the linear conversations!). I know, I know, it's pointless for me to expect both worlds to coexist. After all, if I planted a seed in the soil and it began to grow, I wouldn't expect to find the seed again. I wouldn't dig around looking for it, disrupting the soil, damaging the plant's roots, and stunting its growth. Nor would I expect the plant to look like the seed. Similarly, I can't go back to life before children when my body and schedule were slimmer, my days neater, and my circumstances more predictable. I was like a seed then, but now, Jesus has asked me to lay down my life for my children. I have begun the dying process and there is no turning back.

We are crucified with Christ and we no longer live, but Jesus Christ now lives in us (Gal. 2:20). When you and I look in the mirror, I hope we don't expect to see a seed. I hope we expect to see God at work in the garden of our souls. Life as it was is giving over to life as it is now: messy, yes, but bursting with good fruit.

RECEIVING SELFLESSNESS THAT PRODUCES FRUIT

Something to cherish:
God is able to make all grace abound to you, so that having all sufficiency in all things at all times, you may abound in every good work. . . . He who supplies seed to the sower and bread for food will supply and multiply your seed for sowing and increase the harvest of your righteousness. You will be enriched in every way to be generous in every way, which through us will produce thanksgiving to God.
—2 Corinthians 9: 8, 10–11

Something to sing:
"Sovereign Over Us" by Michael W. Smith

Something to read:
Arrows Make Terrible Crowns by Janet Mylin

Something to consider:

- Can I think of an example of how my "dying to self" in motherhood has produced fruit?

- How does Jesus want me to lay down my life today?

- What will it look like for me to abide in Jesus today?

- How is Jesus producing good fruit in me? Can I pause and thank Him for this?

- What losses do I need to mourn from "before"? What evidence of growth do I need to embrace and enjoy?

MY PRAYER FOR YOU: *May you surrender your life to Jesus and love your child for His sake. May the Holy Spirit tend you like a garden and make your life abound with good fruit. May you "be steadfast, immovable, always abounding in the work of the Lord, knowing that in the Lord your labor is not in vain" (1 Cor. 15:58).*

PART TWO

THE GIFTS

But the fruit of the Spirit is love, joy, peace,
patience, kindness, goodness, faithfulness,
gentleness, self-control; against such things there
is no law. And those who belong to Christ Jesus
have crucified the flesh with its passions
and desires. If we live by the Spirit,
let us also keep in step with the Spirit.

—*Galatians 5:22–25*

Chapter 6

OTHERS-FOCUSED LOVE

My love is frost and cold, ice and snow;
Let his love warm me,
Lighten my burden,
Be my heaven.[10]

—*THE VALLEY OF VISION*

EXPECT GOD TO LOVE YOU AND YOUR CHILD EVERY DAY, NO MATTER WHAT

When our baby girl arrived five weeks early, weighing less than six pounds and experiencing some minor setbacks, she stayed in the NICU until she was strong enough to come home. After several days of bedside visits, the time finally came when I could hold her. I gently lifted her out of the bassinet, draped the monitor cords over the side of a rocking chair, and held her close. She curled up into the tiniest little bundle. A wave of helplessness rushed over me. Oh, how I wanted to give her life-as-it-should-be, but my heart sank as I realized the impossibility. Already—within her first week of life outside the womb—she had suffered the pricks of needles, the invasion of bright lights, the inconvenience of heart monitors, ongoing hunger pangs, and separation from her mother's arms.

Breastfeeding came slowly to us and she was dropping weight quickly. The doctors suggested that I pump milk in between each stressful breastfeeding session so we could also feed her by spoon, cup, or tube. So I sat in a chair by her bassinet and learned how to use an electric breast pump. In my younger days, I would have taken one look at the unwieldy contraption, heard its hypnotic whir, and walked out of the room. But things had changed: I had a daughter now and she needed milk. I held the bottles to my chest and hoped for liquid gold. It would've been nice to have had some privacy, but just then a nurse walked through the room. When she saw me, a warm smile crossed her face and she said something I will never forget. "A mother's love is beautiful. She will do whatever it takes."

Her words got my attention because—first of all, using an electric breast pump doesn't feel beautiful—and second, she included me in a category of women I hoped to join someday: mothers who truly love their children. Until motherhood, love had seemed easy, but now it seemed complicated, costly, and amorphous. How would I even begin? God would have to cultivate love where selfishness and guardedness grew like weeds. I would have to learn love, one wobbly step at a time.

LEARNING TO LOVE

We shouldn't be surprised that we need to learn how to love our children. Maternal love won't always come naturally: we'll need help, instruction, and encouragement along the way. One of the ways God teaches new moms how to love is through older women. In fact, when Paul wrote to Titus, he told him to encourage the older women to "train the young women to love their husbands and children" (Titus 2:4). With my precious baby in my arms, I began watching and listening to older women more keenly. What had they learned about love as they raised their own children? What could they see from their vantage point that I couldn't see from mine?

I wasn't disappointed. Godly, more seasoned women wrapped their arms around me. They carried, calmed, and befriended my children. They gave me whatever I needed to thrive as a mom, like books, music, food, prayer, and a listening ear. From where I stand today, I can confidently say that older women have taught me more about love than I could ever calculate: their practical advice and spiritual insights have shaped my daily habits and given me a vision for the future. In fact, as you read this book, you're hearing from them in every word. I don't know what I'd do without them.

Of course, my greatest mentor has been the Holy Spirit. He began teaching me about love from the get-go, through the long days (and nights) of caring for an infant. I was so sleep-deprived, I could barely remember my own name, but my baby needed to be fed, changed, and cherished around the clock. She needed me to hold her close, look her in the eye, and sing to her. Sometimes I felt like I couldn't go on—like I couldn't possibly change one more diaper or wash one more milk-drenched shirt—but the Holy Spirit urged me on, teaching me that *love can't ignore a person's needs*.[11] He reminded me that He doesn't ignore me when I am spiritually hungry, thirsty, and filthy. Instead, He meets my needs through Christ and is with me around the clock. During the early days of motherhood, the wondrous cross became real to me. If, when I had reached my limit, I would recall God's attentive love for me through Christ, I'd discover the grace to keep going. In the shadow of the cross, I'd grow in love as a mom. It's worth mentioning that, to this day, when I tend to my children's needs out of the wellspring of God's love for me, I experience a deep sense of pleasure and delight. There's nothing quite like it. I think you would agree.

But back to the early days, when love was new and my cooing baby girl grew into a bright-eyed toddler. She was on the go! I had to simultaneously slow down so she could keep up with me *and* quicken my pace so I could keep up with her. During that season, I began thinking about how to grow a strong mother-daughter relationship. Understandably, my daughter loved me on her own toddler terms: it was clear that if I wanted to build a lasting relationship with her, the ball was in my court. The Holy Spirit taught me that *love always takes the initiative.* After all, God always makes the first move: even when we were dead in our sin, He made us alive with Christ (Eph. 2:5). He's pursuing us to this day.

If I wanted a loving relationship with my daughter, I would have to take the initiative too. So, I made room in my schedule for her. I studied her, curious about what made her tick. I got down on her level, entered into her world, and invited her into mine. I told her Bible stories, made kid-friendly recipes, and planned holiday traditions with an eye toward her spiritual well-being and her love of fun. I don't regret a single move I made in her direction.

> *What started as a tiny blossom of love for my little girl has grown, day by day— never perfectly, of course—but has really grown.*

In time, when my daughter and I started to butt heads over car seats, grocery stores, and bedtimes, I learned that *love always forgives.* In moments of anger and tension, I remembered that when His own people were mocking and crucifying Him, Jesus prayed, "Father, forgive them, for they know not what they do" (Luke 23:34). Jesus demonstrates that *love forgives with or without apology.* God forgives us not because we have met certain conditions, nor because we have begged for mercy, nor because He is in a good mood: He forgives us because it's what love *does.*

Despite my long, slow learning curve, God has worked through motherhood to teach me how to love. What started as a tiny blossom has grown, day by day—never perfectly, of course—but has really grown. I need more love for the days ahead because my children will always need something; they'll always want to be pursued and cherished; and they'll always have reason to be forgiven.

Oh, that I would be first in line! Oh, that I wouldn't give up when the going gets rough and that my love for my kids would echo God's love for them! May the words of 1 John 4 burst into life as I raise my children: "Beloved, if God so loved us, we also ought to love one another. No one has ever seen God; if we love one another, God abides in us and his love is perfected in us" (vv. 11–12). Although my sons cannot see God, I hope that they will experience something of His love through my listening ear, ready smile, and willingness to do whatever it takes to maintain our relationship. And although my daughters cannot see God, I hope that they will experience something of His love through my warm embrace, forgiveness, and helping hand. Oh, how I pray for the grace to abide in Christ's love and to do whatever it takes to share His love with my kids.

Can you relate in some way to the wonder of receiving God's love for you and watching your own heart respond in love for your child? I bet if I walked in on your life, I would see you diligently loving your child—maybe not perfectly, but really doing it—and I would smile and say, "A mother's love is beautiful. She'll do whatever it takes."

COMMITTED TO LOVE

The truth of the matter is, while I know how wonderful it is to love my children, I also know how terrible it is to lack love for them. Sometimes sin—and not love—permeates the words I speak and the way I treat my children. Sometimes I feel cranky, detached, and turned off.

My lack of love breaks my heart because it can hurt my children more deeply than almost anything in the world. What do you do when you don't feel love for your own child? How do you choose love anyway?

We find the answer to this common motherhood struggle in the words of Malachi. Four hundred years before Jesus was born, Malachi prophesied, "He will turn the hearts of fathers to their children and the hearts of children to their fathers, lest I come and strike the land with a decree of utter destruction" (Mal. 4:6). Although this prophecy is specifically about the father-child relationship, I see implications for mothers as well, especially when we are tempted to turn away from our kids.

When we put our faith in Jesus, we are healed from the wounds of our own parents' imperfect love. We are called to share this message of hope with our children.

Perhaps you have found yourself rejecting your own child and it breaks your heart. Or perhaps your own mother turned away from you. Perhaps she had poor parenting skills or was even neglectful or abusive. In whatever way you have been hurt, I hope you find comfort in the fact that God grieves over our broken relationships, including our broken relationship with Him. God sent His own Son—whom *He loves perfectly*—to restore our relationships, first with Him and then with other people. Isaiah 53:5 reminds us that "with his wounds we are healed."

When we put our faith in Jesus, we are healed from the wounds of our own parents' imperfect love. We don't have to fear that we won't mother well or that we will inevitably pass on sinful patterns to our own children. In Christ, we are healed from these wounds and we can share this message of hope with our children. I'll never get over the way God sees Jesus' righteousness on our behalf—when we put our faith in Christ, God sees us as perfectly loving moms—and then He gets to work remaking us into His likeness day after day. I've seen God work wonders through four simple steps of faith.

1. Confess your struggle to a praying friend. A few years ago, I shared with a friend, "I'm really struggling to love one of my kids. Do you ever struggle with this? What should I do?" My friend— a wonderful mother of three happy kids—instantly said, "Of course I struggle with that. I can remember times when I didn't love each one of my children." Her honesty and familiarity with the problem put me at ease. She prayed for me, asking God to warm my heart and to give me His love for my child.

2. Ask yourself, "Why don't I love my child?" My friend encouraged me to prayerfully consider why I was struggling to love my child. My lack of love could be due to a wide range of factors like personality differences, environmental stressors, sin issues, or even sheer exhaustion. It took some time, but once I understood why I was struggling, I was able to seek God's help to move forward.

3. **Consider the right response.** The well-known Serenity Prayer has been helpful to many moms—including me. "God grant me the serenity to accept the things I cannot change, the courage to change the things I can, and the wisdom to know the difference."[12]

Sometimes, our struggle will subside if we simply make a change. For example, we may discover that our lack of love is in response to our child's sinful behavior or character flaw. Our negative feelings, then, are a helpful warning sign about something that could jeopardize our child's future. We can ask God to help us courageously shepherd our child's heart and to bless our child with good, lasting growth. In time, we may be able to say something like, "I thought my son would always be angry, but God has transformed him into a self-controlled and gracious young man. I love the person he has become."

Remember that Jesus will save us from our tangled web of broken affection, and will surprise us with love, **true love.** *We don't need to wrangle our fickle hearts into perfect maternal affection: rather, as we walk with Jesus, He will turn the wildest heart toward home.*

Other times, the reason we struggle to love our children may be unchangeable. Maybe we don't like our child's personality, weakness, or hardships. Maybe we are jealous of their strengths. Or maybe we simply don't love them because they require so much time and attention. We can be honest with God. He can handle our most despicable thoughts and give us grace to accept the things we cannot change. Never forget that He can literally replace aversion with affection. It may take time, but God really does renew us with His Word. He really does make us more like Jesus. In time, we may be able to say something like, "I used to be turned off by my daughter's quirks, but now I can see that she's an amazing person made in the image of God. As it turns out, I love her just the way she is."

4. *Consider whether it's a big deal—or not.* I've often misinterpreted my feelings: what I thought was a lack of love for my child was actually a lack of "like" for something my child was doing or something we were going through together. That's a big difference. You may realize the same thing about your own struggle. Maybe what you thought was a big deal isn't, and you can move forward with a fresh dose of perspective.

Other times, a lack of love for a child is a big deal, and we may need help addressing the underlying issues. It may have nothing to do with our child, but instead may point to something in our own hearts. Motherhood has a way of bringing things up from the past, spotlighting our weaknesses, and exposing sinfulness. God works through motherhood to draw our attention to the places in our hearts where we are still captive to sin or crippled by wounds. He wants to enter into those places and set us free. Let's pay attention and invite Him in.

Or maybe we struggle to love a child because they don't love us. Maybe they treat us poorly. It's hard to love someone who ridicules, rejects, and resents you. This struggle is not too difficult for God to redeem. He will show us what to do next. Let's cling to Him as our source of acceptance, approval, and affection. And let's consider inviting someone wise to come alongside as we take another step toward our beloved child.

• • •

I hesitated to write about this because I don't want my children to read it someday and wonder how often I struggled to love them. (It wasn't often, dear ones. I love you with all my heart.) But I decided to address it anyway because you might need to know you're not alone. My children might need to know they're not alone, either. I imagine they feel similarly about *me* from time to time, as they will about their own children. I want us each to remember that Jesus will save us from our tangled web of broken affection, and will surprise us with love, *true love*. We don't need to wrangle our fickle hearts into perfect maternal affection; rather, as we walk with Jesus, He will turn the wildest heart toward home.

RECEIVING OTHERS-FOCUSED LOVE

Something to cherish:

Beloved, if God so loved us, we also ought to love one another. No one has ever seen God; if we love one another, God abides in us and his love is perfected in us. —1 John 4:11–12

Something to sing:

"Runaway" by Jess Ray

Something to read:

The 5 Love Languages of Children: The Secret to Loving Children Effectively by Gary Chapman and Ross Campbell

Something to consider:

- Can I ask the Lord what He loves about me?

- How have I seen Jesus take initiative to build His relationship with me? How have I seen Him meet my needs? How have I seen Him forgive me, whether I apologized or not?

- What's one thing I can do or say to let my child know how special he or she is in God's sight and in mine?

- When my relationship with my child seems broken, what is one step I can take to pursue reconciliation? Who can I invite into this process with me?

MY PRAYER FOR YOU: *May you have the power to know how much God loves you. May you receive His love with wide-open arms. May God's love change the way you see yourself and your child. May it shape your thoughts, the words you speak, and the way you spend your time. May it steady you with a deep sense of purpose. And may your child encounter the love of the Lord Jesus through you.*

Chapter 7

STRENGTH THROUGH JOY

When we are powerless to do a thing,
it is a great joy that we can come
and step inside the ability of Jesus.[13]

—CORRIE TEN BOOM

EXPECT GOD'S JOY TO MAKE YOU STRONG

My sweet baby girl and I were two peas in a pod. She snuggled into my life as if she had always been there. We walked to the park together singing "Let's Go Fly a Kite," and talked about every little thing. By the time she was two years old, she and I would cry together at the ending of Robert McCloskey's *Time of Wonder.* We'd hold our pinkies up during tea parties and make believe "surgeon" by carefully stitching heart-shaped beads into rag dolls. I loved the way she pronounced "pretzels" as "prezzels," the way her hair curled like the feathers of a dove, and the way she danced with unapologetic intensity.

When she was almost three, we welcomed another precious baby girl who, arriving full term, gave me the gift of a normal labor, delivery, and postpartum recovery. Ryan and I were so smitten and so amazed by the comparative ease of a full-term baby that we told everyone she was *perfect*. It took us weeks before we finally broke down and admitted, "Actually . . . she cries a lot."

One day, we discovered that she stopped crying when we played music by Benny Goodman. Thereafter, whenever she began to cry, we'd swaddle her up, play our *Best of* album, and dance around the room to big band music. Maybe that's why my earliest memories of motherhood are accompanied by a frolicking soundtrack of "Sing, Sing, Sing" and "In the Mood."

A DREAM COME TRUE

My two little girls and I embarked on nature hikes, created art projects, and visited neighborhood friends. Those were good days. I often thought of Psalm 113:9, a verse I had cherished when I was begging the Lord to fill my womb: "He gives the barren woman a home, making her the joyous mother of children." As I gathered my daughters in my arms and we squished together on the couch to read a favorite book, I realized the Lord had done this for me. It was a dream come true. I kissed their foreheads, inhaling their scent. These precious little girls brought me so much joy.

And yet, although God had given me a home and children, I returned to Psalm 113:9 with a question: Why were there days when I was *not* a joyous mother? Why were there days when I was, in fact, quite sad? What was I doing wrong? Although motherhood multiplied my joy—our home was warm and glowing with life—it also multiplied my sorrows. Certain motherhood struggles stole my joy and, some days, surrounded me with a fog so thick, I couldn't see clearly to appreciate my long-awaited life as a mom.

Joyous mother? Where was she when I woke up wondering if I had done something wrong or if I had what it took to raise my daughters? Where was she when I compared myself to other moms and felt ashamed next to their success? Where was she when I worried why my daughters weren't as creative, industrious, or independent as other kids? Where was she when I struggled to cherish the gifts God had given me and pined for gifts He had withheld? Joylessness drained me of my strength in motherhood. I dragged myself to the Lord and asked, "Why is the mother in Psalm 113 joyous?"

You may struggle with dark days, too, when your head is down, your spirit low, and your jaw clenched in misery. Though the Bible is replete with commands to rejoice always, you may feel like you simply can't. Like me, you may look at the woman in Psalm 113 and wonder, *What's her secret?*

WHAT *IS* JOY?

When I am struggling with joylessness, I remember what joy is in the first place. John Piper, a pastor and theologian who has studied Christian joy extensively, defines it as "a good feeling in the soul, produced by the Holy Spirit, as he causes us to see the beauty of Christ in the word and in the world."[14] Isn't this definition refreshing? I love how Piper takes our desire for joy seriously and points us in the right direction. We all want to be joyful moms: let's dig into this definition phrase by phrase.

"Joy is a good feeling in the soul..." Joy is not just a concept, but it's a very real thing, taking up emotional space, filling our souls. We feel it. And it feels good. In trial, joy may feel content and focused. In sorrow, joy may feel surrendered and peaceful. In good times, joy may feel lighthearted and happy. We can expect joy to affect our thoughts, mood, facial expressions, and even how we express our personality.

"produced by the Holy Spirit..." Joy isn't just the perk of a good night's sleep or a strong cup of coffee (although I'll take both, please), but it is the work of the Holy Spirit, transforming weary women like you and me into women who have the strength to forge ahead and do what we wouldn't have been able to do on our own. I know now that the woman in Psalm 113 isn't joyful simply because her desires are fulfilled and she has a hardworking husband and adorable children.

A husband and children don't produce joy in a woman's soul: they only shine a spotlight on her need for it. Circumstances— no, not even the sweet embrace of a child—are not what create joy in a mother's heart. God alone turns barren women into mothers, and God alone turns downcast mothers into joyous ones. Knowing that joy is produced by the Holy Spirit helps me know where to turn when I feel joyless: instead of demanding joy from my husband or kids, I can turn to the Holy Spirit with open hands.

> *The only time the world will bring us true joy is when we see God in it.*

"as He causes us to see the beauty of Christ in the Word . . ." As we meditate on Scripture, we consider Jesus of Nazareth, who loves us and gave His life for us. We consider what type of man He is— His character and personality—we consider what type of God He is—His justice and mercy—and our hearts leap for joy. We consider the way He interacts with us according to the same principles and promises we see in His Word and we can't help but rejoice.

"and in the world." The Holy Spirit also produces joy in us when He shows us Jesus' presence in our personal lives and in the world around us. The *only* time the world will bring us true joy is when we see God in it. Isn't it amazing to see Jesus at work with our children? Isn't it amazing to see Him care for the brokenhearted and lowly? Isn't it amazing to see Him dwell in us and sustain us no matter how hard things get?

I once asked a friend who had raised seven children, "What was the best thing about being a mom?" She replied, "When things went right." She rejoiced when her children obeyed, when one child was kind to another, and when she could see God's personal touch in their lives. She agreed with Jesus' disciple, John, who wrote, "I have no greater joy than to hear that my children are walking in the truth" (3 John 4).

I can see what she means. My soul soars when I snuggle my newborn or watch my six-year-old run like the wind. My heart sings when my children pray for one another or help a neighbor. I sigh with deep relief when an argument is transformed into peace, a lie is uprooted by the truth, or a cold heart melts in the warmth of grace. Jesus is in our midst. In these moments, I feel something more than happy; I feel joy.

You and I could be having the hardest day—wading through sickness, crankiness, and mess—and we could turn our eyes to Jesus and find every reason to rejoice. You and I—strong, joyous mothers—could sing with the psalmist,

> *You make known to me the path of life;*
> *in your presence there is fullness of joy;*
> *at your right hand are pleasures forevermore.*
> —Psalm 16:11

CONFRONTING THE THIEVES OF JOY

Yet sometimes joy is elusive and can feel swept away in a quick-rising gust of wind. I have found that joy can be stolen by comparison, mom-guilt, and lack of gratitude.

Comparison. I thought I overcame comparison in middle school, but it came back full force once I became a mom. From the start, I compared the size of my baby bump with those of the women in my Aqua Mom class at the YMCA. I compared my birth story with a friend's adoption story. I compared my postpartum recovery with celebrities' return to normalcy. I compared every aspect of my motherhood with other women.

> *Comparison became a nasty sidekick that followed me everywhere.*

Who bounced back faster? Who got more sleep? Who became a stay-at-home mom? Who returned to work? Who read more books? Who took more nature hikes? Who enjoyed motherhood? Who didn't?

Comparison became a nasty sidekick that followed me everywhere. I would load my kids into the van after a playdate and spend the entire ride home comparing myself with my friends, beating myself up for being too lenient, too overbearing, too underprepared, too attentive, too detached, too attached, too frumpy, too old, and too tired to be a good mom. All this from spending time with friends whom I loved and who were doing a wonderful job parenting their kids. Nonetheless, when I compared myself to them, I lost the joy of friendship and motherhood in one fell swoop. A cloud of despair would settle over me. I'd distance myself from my friends and snap at my kids who were easier to blame than myself.

These days, I still compare myself to other moms. Not much has changed in that regard. However, I'm learning to see myself and other women through God's eyes: each of us is precious and unique; each of us brings strengths and weaknesses into motherhood. I'm learning the redemptive purpose of comparison—to help us see our need for God's saving grace and to help us grow in maturity. As Heather Holleman puts it, "Knowing and enjoying Jesus is the point of the Christian life, and when I lose this essential truth, . . . I will continually compare my life to that of others, imagining their happiness and their joy, while bemoaning my own situation."[15] Moms can learn from one another and lean on one another's strengths. When the adage "comparison is the thief of joy" threatens to be true, let's find our joy in Christ and remember His delight over moms, including you.

Mom-guilt. And then right along with comparison comes the mom-guilt. Who among us has not felt this? Being a mom has brought with it a deluge of accusations: *"I am not enough." "I am too much." "I will never get it together."* Whether I forget to pack my son's snack or overlook a major issue in my daughter's character, mom-guilt spirals quickly into mom-shame. A simple "I forgot something" becomes an agonized "I'm a failure and I'm destroying my child's life." I'm not alone in this and you aren't either:

every mom is pummeled by the weight of her own imperfections from time to time. Mom-guilt is like smog, clouding our vision. And it certainly doesn't solve the problem that led to the guilt in the first place.

Mom-guilt is a lethal combination of self-righteousness and a lack of trust in God's love for us and our children. The question is, what will we do with it? The solution to mom-guilt is twofold. First, we've got to get our eyes off ourselves and stop expecting ourselves to be perfect. Instead, we must look to Jesus and rest in His perfection: "There is therefore now no condemnation for those who are in Christ Jesus" (Rom. 8:1). It's helpful to surround ourselves with friends who will not let us beat ourselves up, but instead will remind us of Christ's forgiveness and grace. And when our friends are caught in mom-guilt, we can hug them and point them to Christ too. If a friend doesn't know Jesus yet, this might be the perfect opportunity to tell her about the One who will replace her shame with joy.

It's helpful to surround ourselves with friends who will not let us beat ourselves up, but instead will remind us of Christ's forgiveness and grace.

The second solution is to trust God to care for our children better than we can. Only God can accommodate our limitations and transform our botched efforts into something good for our kids. Whenever I have negatively impacted my kids and I'm feeling the familiar ache of mom-guilt, I hand the whole mangled mess to our heavenly Father and ask Him to fix it. And He does.

Sometimes He shows me how I can make amends, learn from my mistakes, and move forward, and—more times than I can count—He works things out for the good of my children in ways I hadn't seen coming.

Lack of gratitude. Surprisingly, most of my misery in mother-hood doesn't come from challenging circumstances, but from a third thief of joy: lack of gratitude. This comes up when I'm entrenched in the hard work of caring for my children. Even though my husband also happily takes full responsibility for our kids, there's just something about being the mom. Most days, God gives me the grace to enjoy my calling, but other days, I resent it. I focus on what I lack and what I want, instead of what God has given me.

> *When Jesus suffered, He welcomed His future joy into His present circumstances. This joy gave Him strength to keep going and to complete His mission.*

Discontentment settles over my soul when I least expect it. I may be on vacation in a beautiful place with every convenience in the world; my children may be healthy and cheerful; my husband may be attentive and positive, and yet I begin to feel sorry for myself for having to pack suitcases, plan snacks, and miss out on a fun activity in order to stay back with a napping baby or a tuckered-out toddler. In no time at all, I can create a narrative of self-pity and oppression that clouds over the vacation's happy memories.

Regardless of where or when it happens, my lack of gratitude darkens life for my entire family. I hate it. In those moments, I desperately need the Holy Spirit to give me joy. Things take a turn for the better when I talk to our heavenly Father about my complaints and about the cost of motherhood. As we talk things over, He guides me through the gloom of discontent into the refreshing clarity of gratitude. Sometimes the change occurs instantly; other times it's more like a marathon, but sure enough, God wrenches me out of my selfish misery and nudges me to joyfully embrace the people, work, and life He has given me so generously. I'm always amazed when, moments after sullenly listing the things I lack, I find all my longings met in Christ.

> Let us also lay aside every weight, and sin which clings so closely, and let us run with endurance the race that is set before us, looking to Jesus, the founder and perfecter of our faith, who for the joy that was set before him endured the cross, despising the shame, and is seated at the right hand of the throne of God.—Hebrews 12:1–2

JOY IN TRIAL

What about the times when motherhood is far more difficult than a simple struggle with comparison, mom-guilt, and a lack of gratitude? Can we be joyful in the midst of suffering? Can we find joy in intense and prolonged hardships? These are difficult questions, but I think the answer is *yes*. In trial, the joy of the Lord gives us strength to keep going. The converse is also true in that, as the Lord strengthens and sustains us through trials, we may feel joy simply to see how much He loves us. I can't offer you a formula or a plan other than the encouragement to run to Jesus and rest in His care.

When our heavenly Father asks us to drink a bitter cup, we draw from the depths of what we know of Him: that He will never ask us to suffer a drop more than is necessary for His good purposes. He has weighed every trial in His hand and He will never ask us to bear suffering without Him. We will find reasons to give thanks, even in affliction. This sober and raw gratitude will grow the purest joy, for it will most resemble the suffering of Christ. When Jesus suffered, He welcomed His future joy into His present circumstances. This joy gave Him strength to keep going and to complete His mission. We can do that too.

WHAT GIVES GOD JOY?

Do you know what makes God feel joyful? To answer this question, Jesus told three parables in Luke 15 about people who lost something precious and then found it. Each time, the person rejoices to find the lost treasure. When the lost sheep is found, the owner "lays it on his shoulders, rejoicing" (v. 5); when the lost coin is found, the owner "calls together her friends and neighbors, saying, 'Rejoice with me, for I have found the coin that I had lost'" (v. 9). And when the prodigal son finally returns home, ashamed, trudging down the road, "his father saw him and felt compassion, and ran and embraced him and kissed him.... And they began to celebrate" (vv. 20, 24).

These stories illustrate that whenever one of His precious children is lost in sin, God turns over every rock, shines the searchlight of truth, and does whatever it takes to find us. Then, when we receive His lavish grace, repent of our sin, and return to Him, He embraces us and celebrates joyfully. So, what gives God joy? His children coming home.

Even when you feel joyless, you can lay your weary head on God's shoulder and cherish this: "The LORD your God is in your midst, a mighty one who will save; he will rejoice over you with gladness; he will quiet you by his love; he will exult over you with loud singing" (Zeph. 3:17).

RECEIVING STRENGTH THROUGH JOY

Something to cherish:
You make known to me the path of life; in your presence there is fullness of joy; at your right hand are pleasures forevermore. —Psalm 16:11

Something to sing:
"No One Ever Cared for Me Like Jesus" by Steffany Gretzinger

Something to read:
Loving the Little Years: Motherhood in the Trenches by Rachel Jankovic

Something to consider:

- When have I felt joy through God's Word? When have I felt joy in motherhood?

- In what ways do I struggle with comparison, mom-guilt, or a lack of gratitude? Father, how do You want to change my mind about the things that steal my joy?

- Do I believe that God rejoices over me? Why would He feel this way? How might this truth affect my everyday life? Reread Zephaniah 3:17 and let these amazing phrases sink in.

- How might God's joy strengthen each of these areas of my life? (Jot down a couple of key words and ask the Lord to make them a reality.)

  facial expressions
  tone of voice

atmosphere of our home

impact at my work

my daily choices

schedule

relationships

MY PRAYER FOR YOU: *May the joy of the Lord strengthen you every day. When you compare yourself to other moms, may you grow wiser and more compassionate. May you shed the chains of mom-guilt and wear Christ's righteousness instead. May you be confident in God's ability to care for your child, even when you have messed up. May God bless you with a grateful heart. And may you be a joyous mom.*

Chapter 8

PEACE IN THE UPS AND DOWNS

*May the Lord of peace himself give you
peace at all times in every way.
The Lord be with you.*

—2 THESSALONIANS 3:16

EXPECT JESUS TO BE YOUR PEACE
IN THE STORMS AND IN THE CALM

Life was moving along. I was five months pregnant with our third baby—another sweet baby girl—and beginning to feel her little flutters inside of me. We were moving from our raised ranch in town to a farmette in the country. The big white farmhouse would be the perfect place to raise our growing family. We swooned over the cozy fireplace, the wood floors, and the ample closet space (a rare feature in an old farmhouse). The big girls would share a bedroom and the baby would sleep in a tiny office space next to the master bedroom just waiting to be transformed into a nursery.

Like a dreamy-eyed homesteader, I imagined our three little girls running across the meadow to catch butterflies by day and fireflies by night. I imagined them wading in the creek, eating wild raspberries, and picking juicy tomatoes from the garden. It was picture perfect. Even my due date seemed perfect: October 10, 2010: 10-10-10. I laughed with joy when a friend exclaimed, "Wow. You have a great husband and two beautiful little girls, you're moving to a gorgeous farm, *and* your baby is due on 10-10-10. How perfect is that?"

HEARTBREAK

The day arrived for the baby's twenty-week anatomy scan and we couldn't wait to catch a glimpse of her face and see her kick and wiggle in my womb. We decided to bring the two big girls with us because we thought they would love to see their little sister growing. We crowded into the ultrasound room. I wore a hospital gown and reclined in the examination chair. Ryan stood next to me, holding one little girl in each arm. The technician adjusted the computer screen so we could see it clearly, and moved the ultrasound probe across my belly. An image flickered on the screen. Then, suddenly, the technician turned the screen away.

"I'm so sorry," she said quietly. "Your baby stopped growing."

"What?" I asked, as dread swept over me.

"Your baby has died," she responded in a low voice. "I'm so sorry."

The room was silent. My thoughts were spinning. Ryan leaned in toward me. He and the girls wrapped their arms around my neck. Their bodies pressed into mine as we wept.

• • •

After a while, the doctor came in and talked with us. She said I should go home, pack a bag, and plan to deliver the baby at the hospital the next day. In a cramped ultrasound room, with a darkened computer screen and warm gel on my belly, we were involuntarily welcomed into the sobered group of humanity acquainted with stillbirth.

The next morning, I checked in at the hospital and was led to a room at the end of the labor and delivery hall. I had walked these hallways while laboring with our first two babies. The sights, smells, and sounds reminded me of the excitement of delivering a healthy baby, but I had to override my senses and remind myself, *This is different.* A nurse posted a red leaf on the outside of my door as an unspoken announcement that I was delivering a stillborn baby: *Don't expect an excited mother-to-be. Expect sorrow.*

Doctors and nurses came in, asking me impossible questions.

How did I want to induce labor?

Did I want pain medication?

Did I want visitors?

Did I want to hold the baby when she was delivered?

Did I want to bury or cremate her?

I wanted to scream, "No! I don't want any of these things!"

The doctor said if I took too long to deliver the baby, things could get complicated. She advised me to get out of bed, walk around the room, and do knee-lifts and lunges to speed the contractions. I sat on the edge of the bed, heartbroken, trying to get up the courage to do what I had to do. As I walked around the room, I grimly told myself, *You have to fight your way to the end of this. You have to push yourself toward your greatest fear.*

I had grown accustomed to this baby's presence in my life. I remembered the first few weeks of pregnancy when all I could do was sit on the couch and stare at the wall because I felt so sick. I remembered Mother's Day when the baby seemed to be fluttering and kicking just for me. I remembered the dreams we had been weaving as a family and how they all included our precious little girl. But now I had to say goodbye. As I tried to bring on labor, I pleaded with God for help. It came to mind that sometimes when people are dying, they seem to wait until a loved one releases them.

I placed my hand on my womb.

I knew she had already gone, but I still had to let her go.

I looked down at my round belly and did the last thing I wanted to do.

I said, "You can go now."

• • •

I've always imagined stillbirth as a quiet, sterile experience, but in reality it is full of movement, humanity, and noise—the beating hearts, the agonizing labor and delivery, the guttural cries of despair. The only *stillness*, really, is the precious little body that emerges to say, "I was here. But I am not anymore."

That one little person is so very, very still.

Everyone else keeps pushing forward, groaning and grieving.

• • •

The nurse wrapped our baby girl in delivery blankets and nestled her in the crook of my arm. I untucked the blanket to look at her. She was so little, pink, and fragile. But already, she looked like one of our babies. She even had her great-grandmother's chin. I hadn't expected to feel the same maternal bond I had felt when I held our first two warm and hungry daughters, but I did. I was invaded by love for her. I felt delighted by her—proud of her—*so pleased* by how far she had come. On this side of heaven, she would never grow to be more than a tiny, still body, yet I loved her with all my heart.

The hospital sent me home with a small cream-colored box. In it, they placed a stuffed bear, a gold ring that fit around her arm, and a bracelet with her name spelled out in tiny, iridescent beads: *Juliette Abigail.* This was all I had of my beloved child, all I had to touch, look at, and hold close.

LIFE GOES ON

A few days later, we moved to the farmhouse, but it was not the picture-perfect scene I had imagined. Instead of digging in the dirt to plant tomatoes, we dug a tiny grave. Instead of running in the meadow, our girls placed rosebuds on a cedar box and said goodbye to their sister. Instead of moving the crib into the new nursery, Ryan and his friends somberly carried it up to the attic. People brought meals. Friends unpacked boxes. In the days that followed, I mustered up the courage to ask my friends, "Do you want to see my keepsakes?" We would sit together on the front porch where I'd open the cream-colored box and take out each item representing Juliette: the teddy bear, the ring, and the bracelet. I missed her so much.

It took a while for life to go on. For months, everything seemed uncertain. Losing Juliette meant I could lose any one of my children at any time. If I couldn't protect a baby tucked inside my body, how could I protect my daughters who were running, jumping, and exploring? How could I protect future pregnancies? Would they end in stillbirth too? And why did the stillbirth occur? Was I sick? Had I done something wrong? Had I given up too easily? I felt helpless. Tossed at sea.

You might wonder if stillbirth shook my faith, if it destroyed my sense of peace and made me doubt God's love. At times it did. You might wonder if I felt abandoned, lonely, and vulnerable; if I saw God as heartless, vindictive, or careless. At times I did. But ultimately, losing Juliette solidified my faith in God's love for me and taught me peace in the middle of the storm.

GOD IS OUR ROCK, AND THERE IS NO UNRIGHTEOUSNESS IN HIM

There are certain things I wish I had known about stillbirth while I was going through it, but I was in the dark. I didn't even know what to pack in my hospital bag. I wish I had packed my camera. (These were the days before cellphone cameras.) I wish I had packed a large pillow to hold in my arms when they discharged me from the hospital and pushed my wheelchair through the corridors to the exit. It would have been nice to have something to fill the void in my arms and to sit on my lap where—after a healthy birth—a new mom holds an infant car seat with a beautiful, chubby newborn tucked inside. When people heard my wheelchair coming from the labor and delivery wing, they looked at me expectantly. They looked for an infant car seat and then quickly looked away when all they saw was a small, cream-colored box.

Although I hadn't packed everything I would have wanted, God had carefully prepared me for this tragedy in the most surprising way: He got a children's song stuck in my head. From the moment the ultrasound technician lowered her eyes, to the moment—many months later—when I was finally able to wake up with a smile, the version of Psalm 92:15 from the ministry Songs for Saplings played in my mind repeatedly. I didn't conjure it up or choose to meditate on it, but it stubbornly shaped my stream of consciousness and accompanied every thought: "He is my rock, and there is no unrighteousness in him." As it turns out, this truth was exactly what I needed.

God provided this verse to be like a lifeboat for my sinking ship. I had come to expect storms in motherhood, but stillbirth really took me under. The waves arched above my head and my feet were knocked out from under me. Any false confidence I had placed in myself was exposed, devastated, and washed away to sea. I'd shake my fist at heaven and cry, "It's not supposed to be like this!" I fought the storm for days, weeks. My quavering voice would be swallowed by the thrum of Psalm 92:15, "He is my rock, and there is no unrighteousness in him."

God does not play games with our lives. He will never allow harm to befall me or my family unless He plans to redeem it for a good so glorious as to render past sorrows obsolete. And nothing—not even this tragedy—can snatch me out of His hand.

Like a first responder, the Holy Spirit was using Psalm 92:15 to call through the storm, "God is *for* you! Be held by Him!" Finally, exhausted, I stopped fighting against the storm and turned my ear toward His call. Sure enough, He was there.

God was my rock: there for the claiming, there for the clinging to, there as a place to gasp for air, and there to heave my sorrows upon. I could throw my full weight on Him and He would bear it. He would not slip away in the night and leave me to perish.

And God was righteous. Though stillbirth felt so evil—so unrighteous—I clung to the truth that there is no unrighteousness in God. Juliette did not die because God had a lapse in judgment. She did not die because He was cruel or vindictive. God does not play games with our lives. He doesn't operate on superstition. Nor is He swayed by money, power, or pleasure the way humans are. On the contrary, He is fettered by His own goodness and fully satisfied by Christ's death on the cross. He will never allow harm to befall me or my family unless He plans to redeem it for a good so glorious as to render past sorrows obsolete. And nothing—not even this tragedy—can snatch me out of His hand (John 10:27–30).

If I learned anything from losing Juliette, I learned that God is close to the brokenhearted. And that He is our rock—a righteous Savior. Even when the storms of life are raging around us, we can lay our heads back and trust Him.

JESUS IS YOUR PEACE IN THE CALM

How reassuring. Christ alone is our peace in the storms of motherhood. And He alone is our peace when motherhood is relatively calm and we simply face the conflicts of everyday life with kids.

God's peace is meant to transform our daily lives as we dwell in our earthly homes with our earthly children. It isn't some castle-in-the-sky promise for the future. In fact, you and I can pursue the peace of God in motherhood by taking three steps of faith from Philippians 4:5–9. It'll be well worth our time to prayerfully consider practicing these beautiful things as we raise our kids.

*The Lord is at hand; do not be anxious about anything, but in everything **by prayer and supplication with thanksgiving*** *let your requests be made known to God. And the peace of God, which surpasses all understanding, will guard your hearts and your minds in Christ Jesus. . . . Whatever is true, whatever is honorable, whatever is just, whatever is pure, whatever is lovely, whatever is commendable, if there is any excellence, if there is anything worthy of praise,* **think about these things.** *What you have learned and received and heard and seen in me—* **practice these things,** *and the God of peace will be with you.*

Peace-filled moms give thanks in prayer. Can I be honest? Even though I love peace, I often get caught up in the noisy whirlwind of life-with-kids and can't find my way out. I give in to chaos. (Not to mention, I often create chaos.) In those moments, I want to be a peacemaker, but I can't do it alone. I need God's help. Maybe you can relate. This passage in Philippians is good news for us because it promises that God's peace will protect our thoughts and emotions even when the world—or the room—around us is in an uproar. According to Philippians 4, whenever you and I pray with thanksgiving, we can count on God's peace to stand up like a bodyguard, flex its muscles, and take its stand between us and our circumstances.

> **We are doing much more than positive thinking: we are gearing up to face every circumstance in motherhood with the unshakeable peace of God.**

We need grace-filled humility and grit to face our circumstances, tell the Lord what we need, and thank Him. The Prince of Peace, who created us with hearts and minds that work best when in communion with Him, will help us walk in the light of Philippians 4 and will protect us with His peace.

Peace-filled moms think well. God wants us to feed our faith and not our fear. He wants us to think about things that are true, honorable, just, pure, lovely, commendable, excellent, and worthy of praise. By exercising our minds in this way, we are doing much more than positive thinking: we are gearing up to face every circumstance in motherhood with the unshakeable peace of God. When our thoughts are grounded in truth, we can be effective in chaos and reasonable in conflict. We can process bad news. We can work on rocky relationships. We can meet threatening circumstances with bravery.

Though my circumstances hadn't changed, my thoughts did. In the worst of circumstances, I could thank God for His great love for me.

The pursuit of peace starts in our minds and then moves outward, transforming our everyday lives. My friend Lauren says that when the walls seem to be closing in on her, she and her kids head out the door. The thrill of adventure and the beauty of creation shift their perspective and help them remember God. So, in the summer, you'll find them at the creek with inflatable rafts and a picnic lunch. In the winter, you'll find them at the largest sledding hill in town or treading through the foam pit at the local gym. Lauren invites friends so we can all enjoy the camaraderie and seek the peace of God together. I love joining in whenever we can because initiating adventure is not my go-to.

When the walls are closing in on me and my kids are bouncing off of them, I play music. We may be irritable or out of control, but when Elizabeth Mitchell or JJ Heller starts singing, we breathe a sigh of relief and find something productive to do. My other go-to is to cuddle up with my kids to read aloud. Entering into a world of interesting characters, high-stakes decisions, delightful language, and a rousing triumph of good over evil is usually just what we need to think well and experience the peace of God.

Peace-filled moms make peace. Thankfully, God's peace doesn't stop with us, but flows out of us and onto our kids. We become peacemakers, Christ's ambassadors (2 Cor. 5:20–21). When our children are shaken by trials, we can hold them close and remind them of God's character. When they struggle with sin, we can remind them of God's offer of salvation. When their relationships are a mess, we can coach, mediate, and pray for peace. With God's help, you and I can build homes where repentance, forgiveness, and reconciliation are the norm. Instead of sowing seeds of strife, we can sow seeds of peace that will grow and produce a harvest of righteousness.

• • •

I've never asked my friends and family if they noticed a marked difference in me after October 10, 2010—the date once marked with the hope of a baby but then marked by loss—but I've always imagined that they would say God entered my sorrow and filled my empty arms with a tangible gift: His *peace*.

RECEIVING PEACE IN THE UPS AND DOWNS

Something to cherish:
You keep him in perfect peace whose mind is stayed on you, because he trusts in you. Trust in the LORD forever, for the LORD GOD is an everlasting rock. —Isaiah 26:3–4

Something to sing:
"Your Hands" by JJ Heller

Something to read:
When Life and Beliefs Collide by Carolyn Custis James

Something to consider:

- Where in your life do you need God's peace right now?

- What practices can you adopt to experience His peace?

MY PRAYER FOR YOU: *I pray that you would not have storms in motherhood, but if you do, may you cling to the Rock. May you receive God's peace and know how much He cares about you in motherhood's ups and downs. May you practice true gratitude as you present your requests in prayer and welcome life-giving thoughts into your heart and mind. May you practice peacemaking with your own child, knowing you are a beloved child of a peacemaking God.*

Chapter 9

PATIENCE IN TRIAL

*I realized that the deepest spiritual lessons
are not learned by His letting us have our
way in the end, but by His making us wait,
bearing with us in love and patience until we
are able to honestly pray what He taught
His disciples to pray: Thy will be done.*[16]

—ELISABETH ELLIOT

EXPECT GOD TO WAIT FOR YOU
AND HELP YOU WAIT FOR HIM

Days after burying Juliette, we traveled out of town to visit my family for Father's Day. We were late to church and our seats were uncomfortably close to the front. As we slid into place, the pastor was calling out the names of fathers whose wives had delivered babies that year. One by one, the happy fathers came forward and accepted a pound of flavored coffee. When the pastor finished reading through his list of names, he held out another bag of coffee. With a warm smile, he said, "One bag left. Any other fathers out there whose wives delivered a baby or are expecting a baby this year?"

Ryan and I leaned into each other and sat, silently. We could not claim the coffee. This was a celebration of receiving children and we couldn't blanket it with our loss, but in our hearts, we cried out, "We did. We delivered a baby this year. Her name is Juliette and she is beloved. We did." A lump rose in my throat as sorrow invaded an otherwise pleasant Sunday. My sister and her husband—sitting next to us—had recently discovered they were expecting a baby, but they didn't claim the coffee either. Though they were delighted about their baby, they were also sorrowful about ours. We all just sat in silence. What is a person supposed to do when sorrow and joy mingle? Their bittersweet union is beyond human understanding. Their heartrending dance silences the room. All we could do was gasp for breath under the weight of their entwined hands, believing that at the end of the dance, joy takes the final bow.

LIGHT AND HEAVY SORROWS

When I was growing up, I daydreamed about the brother I almost had. I was certain he would have been handsome, funny, and strong. He would have protected me and saved the day. He would have invited his friends over to watch movies on Friday nights. Those big, lanky boys would've slung arms around each other and told funny jokes. When I would emerge from my reverie, I'd sigh, "Oh, well. He was never born."

I was basing my daydream on a baby who died when my mom was four months pregnant. The delivery doctor had said something about the baby being "incompatible with life." Despite the doctor's conclusion, I still wondered, "What if the baby had made it? What if he had been a boy and I actually had a brother?"

At the time, I didn't understand the implications of the fact that I was born nine months after he died. There I was, imagining his blond hair and goofy grin, totally missing one vital detail. On this earth—on this side of heaven—he and I could not have existed side by side. We never would have wrestled or joked. He never would have introduced me to his friends. For reasons beyond my comprehension, God created me when someone else died. He made me compatible with life when someone else was not. I have a name, a fingerprint, and my own allotted days on earth. After a season of sorrow, God gave my parents joy. He gave them a baby and it happened to be me.

We might not describe light irritations as "sorrows," but if we take a closer look, we see them for what they are: the thorns and thistles of a broken world.

A timeline stretches from each point of sorrow to its corresponding point of joy when our suffering is resolved. As we wait, we are practicing a precious fruit of the Spirit: patience.

Sometimes our motherhood sorrows are light. The time we wait for their resolution is brief: maybe our baby has a blow-out diaper just as we are heading out the door or maybe our newborn won't fall asleep on the very night we were hoping to meet up with some friends. Maybe our toddler refuses to put on his shoes, our preschooler insists on another cookie, or our kindergartner interrupts an important phone call. Perhaps our sixth grader can't find his baseball uniform, our high schooler forgets to hang up her bath towel, or our college student refuses to attend office hours even though it would improve his grades. We might not describe these irritations as "sorrows," but if we take a closer look, we see them for what they are: the thorns and thistles of a broken world. They get in our way, muck up our schedule, and hold us back from the good life. They are low-grade sorrows, making us feel impatient to get back to business, to move along. We want things to go the way we want them to go. We want people to do the things we want them to do. We want motherhood's everyday sorrows to give way to joy.

Other times, our motherhood sorrows are grievous and long-lasting. Maybe our newborn is sick and the doctors can't figure out why or our toddler isn't speaking and the speech therapist is stumped. Perhaps our kindergartner is sexually abused or our sixth grader is bullied. Maybe our high schooler struggles with anxiety or our adult daughter stays in an unhealthy relationship because she can't see her own immeasurable worth. These things are wretchedly painful, and we would do anything to relieve our children from such suffering. We sit in agony and ask, "How long, O Lord? How long?"

Every mom is well acquainted with the visceral invasion of impatience. We may pray, strategize, push against the boundaries, and grit our teeth to move things ahead, but when things don't change, we're tempted to explode. Of course, none of us wants to be so easily ignited. None of us wants to hurt our children with impatience or irritability. To help us endure this intense motherhood trial, God gives us the gift of patience. Whether we are waiting for something extraordinary like the arrival of a baby or something ordinary like our child to stop wetting the bed, patience grows in us as we surrender our own agenda to God's and wait for Him to resolve the sorrows of life.

AT THE FEET OF JESUS

We see patience in full display as a crowd presses up against Jesus in Luke 8. The crowd is packed with suffering people, all hoping Jesus will replace their sorrow with joy by healing, delivering, feeding, or teaching them.

In this scene, a man named Jairus makes his way through the crowd and falls at Jesus' feet, imploring Him to come to his house because his twelve-year-old daughter is dying, and he desperately needs Jesus to come quickly and heal her. At the same time, a woman who has had a chronic discharge of blood for twelve years approaches Jesus from behind. She has tried all other remedies and sought help from many doctors, but nothing has made a difference. Out of desperation, she reaches out and touches the fringe of

Jesus' garment, and she is healed instantly. Jesus stops in His tracks, turns around, and looks for this woman in the midst of the crowds.

Peter impatiently tries to move Jesus along, saying, "Master, the crowds surround you and are pressing in on you!" (v. 45), but Jesus continues looking for her. Finally, He sees her. Realizing she is not hidden from Him, the woman approaches Him again "and falling down before him [declares] in the presence of all the people why she had touched him, and how she had been immediately healed" (v. 47).

She had waited twelve years for this. Jesus is not rushed by the crowd. He isn't swayed by the crowd's demands or agenda. Instead, He entrusts their needs and the timing of His ministry to His heavenly Father. For the moment, connecting with this one precious woman is His work. He looks at her and blesses her, saying, "Daughter, your faith has made you well; go in peace" (v. 48). What joy she must have felt!

By now, we may have forgotten the other person imploring Jesus for help in this scene. Jairus is still waiting for Jesus to come to his house and heal his daughter. But while Jesus is taking His time to bless the woman, someone comes from Jairus's house to tell him that his daughter has already died. Can you imagine his devastation? Can you imagine what anguish he must have felt as his sorrow mingled with someone else's joy? I wonder if he began to question Jesus' intentions. I wonder if he began to question Jesus' power. If Jesus couldn't show up when a Messiah was needed, who could? Have you ever been in a similar situation in which you have desperately needed God's help in a trial or temptation, but He didn't seem to show up? I have.

Has your sorrow ever mingled with someone else's joy? Mine has.

In that moment, Jesus moves His attention toward Jairus, saying, "Do not fear; only believe, and she will be well" (v. 50). Then He walks to Jairus's house where He is met by yet another crowd, this one mourning for the child. Jesus says to them, "Do not weep, for she is

Jesus always arrives and He is always on time. Though we cannot foresee or understand His method, we can expect Him to rescue us from sorrow at just the right time.

not dead but sleeping" (v. 52). They laugh at Him because they know that she is dead and He is too late. God's timing has failed them. But the next few verses finish the story in triumph. Jesus approaches the bed where the little girl is lying, holds her hand, and says, "Child, arise" (v. 54). Her spirit returns. In fact, she pops right up just as you'd expect a spunky twelve-year-old to do.

Jesus tells her parents to give her something to eat. Luke writes, "Her parents were amazed" (v. 56) and no wonder: when Jairus was waiting for Jesus to come to his house, it didn't seem like Jesus knew what He was doing. It didn't seem like His plan was good or His character trustworthy. But Jesus arrived at the house of mourning just in time. He took a little girl by the hand and restored a family that had been weeping one moment, and the next moment was rummaging through the pantry for the makings of a feast. Jesus always arrives, and He is always on time.

WHEN YOU ARE IMPATIENT . . .

Is there hope for moms like me who struggle with impatience? Yes, there is hope. Jesus patiently endured the cross so that you and I could have His mindset about time. One of the most effective things we can do as moms is to trust God to establish our work for us, moment by moment. Whenever we feel impatient, we can take the inner posture of Jairus or of the woman who was healed and we can press in to Jesus. In motherhood, I run up against countless opportunities to lose my cool, but I'm learning to pause and open my hands, literally or in my mind's eye, and surrender to God's sovereign will. Time after time, He gives me the grace to make the most of my circumstances. It's not fancy, but for me, this is how patience grows.

So, here's what I recommend: when your child derails you, ask your heavenly Father to recalibrate your will to align with His. He will help you keep time as He does, see your child through His eyes, and be a source of blessing even while you wait for resolution. He'll help you to build your relationship with your child and value the work He has given you to do, even if it's not what you were hoping to do today. What if you're late for an important appointment? What if your unplanned circumstances have major consequences? I tell you with all my heart that the God of the universe will work things out for the woman who surrenders control into His capable hands. It may not play out as you had imagined, but it will be far better. He will help you to face whatever comes next, step by step.

• • •

I wonder if my daughters ever think about their sister Juliette. I wonder if they imagine her free spirit, her long brown hair, and her funny antics. I wonder if they daydream about singing and shopping together, sharing book recommendations, and helping each other on projects. The thing they may not understand is that nine months after Juliette's due date, I gave birth to their brother. The months in between Juliette's death and his birth were fraught with fear and impatience. I often knelt before the Lord, pleading for Him to come to my house of mourning and make things turn out right. I had to practice patience. Then, one balmy midsummer day, I gave birth to a robust baby boy who lay on my stomach, skin-to-skin, squinting his eyes and looking up at me like the sweetest thing.

Today, our son is a vibrant ten-year-old. I ruffle his hair and tell him I love him simply because he's my son. I tell him I loved him *long* before he could hit a baseball, build a robot, or eat an entire muffin in one bite. He's an absolute delight, and I wouldn't trade him for anything. Yet I will always miss his big sister Juliette. The whole, mysterious story makes me long for the day when Jesus will return to our worldwide house of mourning, wipe every tear from our eyes, and restore joy to the world. May God give us patience in the waiting.

RECEIVING PATIENCE IN TRIAL

Something to cherish:

I waited patiently for the LORD; he inclined to me and heard my cry. —Psalm 40:1

Something to sing:

"His Eye Is on the Sparrow" by Charles Gabriel

Something to read:

Every Bitter Thing Is Sweet: Tasting the Goodness of God in All Things by Sara Hagerty

Something to consider:

- Will I ask Jesus to give me the courage to push through the crowded places in my heart, and bow at His feet and touch His hem?

- When do I typically feel impatient with my child? How can I reach out to Jesus for patience in those moments?

- Am I enduring any grim trials? Sorrows? Hardships? How can I take heart and wait for God to do something good through this?

MY PRAYER FOR YOU: *When life is not going according to plan, may you press in to Jesus. May you open your hands in surrender, knowing that He will hear you, heal you, and help you. May you become more patient with yourself and your child, knowing that your heavenly Father is patient with you too.*

Chapter 10

KINDNESS TOWARD CHILDREN

Three things in human life are important:
The first is to be kind.
The second is to be kind.
And the third is to be kind.[17]

—HENRY JAMES

EXPECT GOD'S KINDNESS
TO MELT YOUR HEART

Fast-forward several years down the road when we had four adorable kiddos and had just returned from the Christmas tree farm. The kids were bubbling with excitement. We took off hats, gloves, and boots and warmed up by the fire while Ryan propped the tree in the living room and snipped the twine that was wound around the limbs. We all cheered as the tree opened to its original shape. The kids inhaled the tree's piney scent and took turns twirling in the tree skirt. Needless to say, my energy level did not match theirs.

Trekking through the rolling hills of Fraser firs with energetic ten-, seven-, four-, and one-year-olds—while managing morning sickness (I had just discovered that I was pregnant)—had worn me out. I only wanted to put my feet up. As I sat on the couch, I reviewed my holiday to-do list: in the days to come, we would celebrate Advent, hang twinkle lights, read holiday books, bake cookies, shop for presents, make presents, wrap presents, watch movies, and listen to hours of Christmas music. That's when I remembered I had also agreed to help organize a children's choir to sing at the Christmas Eve service. I was in over my head.

A BREAKTHROUGH REHEARSAL

We often participated in the Christmas Eve service at our church, and this year, Ryan and I were organizing a children's choir to sing "Jesus, Joy of the Highest Heaven." My first task was to teach the song to our children so they could sing confidently when we gathered the rest of the choir for rehearsal.

Our ten- and seven-year-old daughters learned it immediately. Their sweet voices lilted like angels. Our four-year-old, on the other hand, struggled to remember the words no matter how hard he tried. We would get three measures into the song and he would collapse to the floor in big, boo-hoo tears because he had forgotten the words. Our one-year-old fussed through the whole song, wanting to sit on my lap, play the piano, empty the closet, eat a snack, drink some milk, and take a nap all at the same time. My memory could be playing tricks on me, but I'm pretty sure this happened every time we gathered around the piano to sing. I lost my patience on more than one occasion. I'd clench my jaw and bribe the little ones to stop crying for *one blessed minute*. It was never the homey "I'll-be-home-for-Christmas" scene you may imagine.

But one rehearsal was different from all the rest. As usual, my four-year-old was crying, my one-year-old was screaming, and the girls, quite discouraged, were furtively watching for my reaction. We were all fed up with one another and

Every day, God lavishes us with kindness—from the rising of the sun, to the food we eat, to the voices we employ. As I played the piano and the chaos continued, I knew Jesus was in our midst.

the moment was anything but holy, but this time I was listening to the lyrics. The older girls sang about our precious Lord Jesus who came as a helpless baby, crying, and needing His mother to hold Him. He came sharing our smiles and tears, hungering for relationship, and facing all manner of danger. They sang about how Jesus came to take away our darkness and transform us from strangers into children of God.

In the cacophony, the Holy Spirit reminded me that God was being kind to us when He sent Jesus to share our human struggle.

He was being kind when He offered to remove our sin from us as far as the east is from the west. As I played the piano and the chaos continued, I knew Jesus was in our midst, supporting us in our flailing attempt to create something beautiful. He was sustaining us when we botched it all up.

Caught up in the truth of the song, I smiled and raised my voice above the din to say, "Keep singing, girls. Jesus came for moments just like this one." Fortified by my encouragement, the girls sang the rest of the song with gusto. I played the melody with my right hand and wrapped my left arm around my teary four-year-old and hungry one-year-old, who continued to cry until the end of the song. I played the final chord and hugged all four of them, thanking God for His kindness in sending Jesus as a baby, for us.

This wasn't the first or the last time God lavished me with kindness in motherhood. In fact, if I had to identify the source of my well-being in motherhood, I would point to God's kindness. Every day—from the rising of the sun, to the food we eat, to the voices we employ—God's kindness makes us flourish. It transforms homes into havens and makes life worth living. The psalmist said this sole attribute of God's is better than life itself: "Because thy lovingkindness is better than life, my lips shall praise thee" (Ps. 63:3 KJV).

RECEIVE GOD'S KINDNESS

Caring for a child day after day exposes a woman's limitations: we simply do not have what it takes to be kind around the clock.

Motherhood opens our eyes to our own childlike nature and the way in which we need someone older, wiser, and stronger to take pity on us and care for us. Our heavenly Father sees our needs and runs to our side.

> As a father shows compassion to his children,
>   so the LORD shows compassion to those who fear him.
> For he knows our frame;
>   he remembers that we are dust.
> —Psalm 103:13–14

Just as we clothe and feed our children, God clothes and feeds us, literally and spiritually. He clothes us in Christ's righteousness and feeds us with the Word of God. We could identify countless parallels between the way we care for our kids and the way God cares for us. From the way He corrects us when we're wrong to the way He develops our gifts and helps us grow, He constantly reminds us that

God remembers what we're made of: dust and divine breath.

we are precious to Him. Even when I lose sight of my fragility— when I foolishly aspire to perfection; when I get caught up in the demands of being an adult; when I overcommit and underdeliver—God smiles on me with compassion and remembers what I'm made of: dust and divine breath.

BESTOW GOD'S KINDNESS

God's kindness toward us enables us to be kind to our children who rely on us to meet their basic human needs, to tell them about God, and to help them along their way. Jesus inspires us to get down on our children's level and empathize with their human struggle. An important part of kindness is remembering that, like us, our children fight a hard battle against their sinful nature. They, too, have an enemy of their souls and are up against a fallen world. But, unlike us, they don't know how to make sense of the battle yet. They don't know about the armor of God—how to wear the helmet of salvation and wield the sword of the Spirit— or about Jesus, our refuge. They don't know about the promise of heaven. They need us to fight on their behalf in the spiritual realm and help them understand the cosmic battle between good and evil as it is taught in the Bible. They need us to take up their cause and guide them faithfully to Christ.

I'm constantly asking God to transform me into a mother who reaches out and nourishes her children with kindness. If kindness is something we can choose—something we can put on like clothing (as the Bible says it is)—then let's choose it! Let's wear it every day and give our kiddos a glimpse of God's heart.

THE WAITRESS DILEMMA

I struggle with what I call the Waitress Dilemma. It happens when I expect my children to pay me back for my kindness. I may smile sweetly and serve patiently all day, but by the evening, I reach my limit and need to be reimbursed. Suddenly, I feel very much like they have been sitting in my roadside diner and ordering free refills all day. I slap down a bill and expect them to pay up. My smile disappears and I demand appreciation.

But this is not the nature of God's lovingkindness: He smiles on us and serves us. His kindness is not deterred by our lack of attention or gratitude toward Him. This is the type of kindness I want to give my kids. So I'm learning how to be kind without keeping an itemized list of my good deeds or a running total of my child's debt. I've asked the Holy Spirit to warn me when I am about to demand payback. He's teaching me to pause and examine what went wrong in my thinking: Was I being kind because the love of Christ compelled me, or was I motivated by applause or appreciation?

I'm also learning the importance of deciding what I am willing to give and what I'm not willing to give. If I am "being kind" and giving my kids whatever they want because they are whining, I end up feeling bitter. But if I am being kind because I chose to be kind, I feel cheerful. A mom with clear boundaries can be kind with all her heart (2 Cor. 9:7).

At times, kindness drains me even when I am doing it for all the right reasons. Can you relate? When we've done the hard work of being kind to our children, we can return to our heavenly Father for refreshment. He will let us know how delighted He is and He'll fill our cup once again.

Our world celebrates public achievement and epic accomplishments, so we might lose sight of motherhood's many uncelebrated opportunities to shape our child's life through kindness. Being a mom has taught me that small acts of kindness make a difference. For example, when I smile, my kids smile too. (In fact, I'm convinced that, besides praying, smiling is the most powerful thing I do as a mom.) When I offer an encouraging word, share a treat, or admire a project, my children seem to breathe a sigh of relief and lean into God's love for them. It's quite amazing. My small-scale choices seem to touch the depths of my children's souls where I cannot go otherwise.

Kindness demands our time and attention; it takes great patience and endurance, but it is the secret to a life well lived.

In God's economy, kindness matters: the details may be small, the acts themselves may be small, and our children may be small, but God will use your kindness to shape your child's entire story. After all, kindness is the language of love. A kind mother will not come up empty-handed. Nor, of course, will her child.

KIND CHILDREN

Perhaps kindness is one of the first and greatest lessons we'll teach our kids. They'll learn the importance of kindness—and how to be kind—from our tone of voice, our words, our facial expressions, and our touch. They'll learn more about kindness from receiving one warm word or one thoughtful gesture from us than they will from a thousand lectures.

When it comes to teaching my children to be kind, my least effective moments are when I get mad at them for failing to be kind. I know this sounds terrible, but sometimes when one child has hurt another child, I immediately attack the child who did the hurting and demand, "What did you do? Why didn't you say you are sorry? Why didn't you show compassion?" Forced kindness never works. I'm more effective when I wrap my arms around *both* kids, suggesting something we could do for the one who was injured. Saying, "Let's go get an ice pack," is a poignant lesson in kindness. What a difference this approach makes

Meanness can grow like a weed when it isn't addressed by a prayerful, compassionate mom.

to all three of us. I'm also learning how to model kindness for my kids by inviting them to join me in visiting someone who is lonely, remembering someone who feels forgotten, and being available to someone who could use a helping hand. Instead of expecting my kids to muster up kindness on their own, I'm learning to welcome my kids to join me as I reach out to those in need.

That's not to say that our kids' actions don't matter. On the contrary, they matter greatly. As their mothers, we must slow down and pay attention to what our children are doing: their actions indicate the condition of their hearts. Meanness can grow like a weed when it isn't addressed by a caring mom. One of my favorite Bible passages is a poem crafted by a mother to teach her son the importance of kindness. She cares very deeply about what her son is doing with his actions, words, and affection.

Notice that she asks him *three times* what he is doing.

> *What are you doing, my son? What are you doing, son of my*
>   *womb?*
> *What are you doing, son of my vows?*
> *Do not give your strength to women,*
>   *your ways to those who destroy kings.*
> *It is not for kings, O Lemuel,*
>   *it is not for kings to drink wine,*
>   *or for rulers to take strong drink,*
> *lest they drink and forget what has been decreed*
>   *and pervert the rights of all the afflicted....*
> *Open your mouth for the mute,*
>   *for the rights of all who are destitute.*
> *Open your mouth, judge righteously,*
>   *defend the rights of the poor and needy.*
> —Proverbs 31:2–5, 8–9

Although the mother seems to be addressing an older son in this passage, the heart of her message is applicable to children of all ages. Her warning about distractions—like wine and infidelity—can be applied to a younger child's propensity toward greed and selfishness. She advises her son to shift his focus from himself to others: to speak up for people who cannot defend themselves, to protect people who are helpless, and to treat all people with dignity. We can nurture these values in our children at any age by teaching them to protect the young, respect the old, and be kind to everyone.

The rest of Proverbs 31 continues the themes of speaking kindly and caring for other people at home and abroad every day. Imagine a family working together to alleviate the suffering of people who are poor and oppressed.

This heartfelt encouragement reminds me how important it is to cast a vision for my kids; to let God's kindness shape their daily choices and life story. Perhaps it begins by making sure our kids spend time with kind people of all ages and walks of life. We can also grow their appetite for kindness through books, music, education, and entertainment that demonstrates the heart of Christ and the dignity of humanity. By God's grace, our efforts to foster kindness in our children will follow them through life.

It's no small thing to be kind. Kindness causes people to flourish as rain showers the earth.

It's no small thing to be kind—to take care of one's family, church members, coworkers, and neighbors—to feed and clothe them and give them courage for the future. Kindness causes people to flourish as rain showers the earth.

• • •

Don't ask me how we all arrived at church on Christmas Eve wearing festive dresses and sweater vests and most of our shoes on, but we did. Our bellies were full and warmed by our traditional Christmas Eve shepherd's meal of soup and bread. The sanctuary glowed with soft candlelight as the children took their places onstage for the opening song. Before walking up to direct the choir,

I tucked our sleepy one-year-old in Grandmom's arms where she snuggled in contentedly. The song began and I looked over the faces of the children in the choir. Our older daughters stood in the back row and sang with all their might. Our brave four-year-old stood in the front row and, yes, forgot the words, and yes, began to cry, but stopped himself, put his shoulders back, and sang the rest of the song. There was no doubt about it, this Christmas Eve sparkled with the kindness of a Savior come to earth to serve His hungry, fragile children and give them life. This time, the only person crying through the entire song was me.

• • •

Oh, by the way, six months later, in the middle of the summer when we weren't singing Christmas carols anymore, guess who suddenly began singing "Jesus, Joy of the Highest Heaven" from beginning to end? Guess who proceeded to sing that carol for a full year as her anthem, her bedtime song, and her swinging song? That precious one-year-old. She'd been listening the whole time.

RECEIVING KINDNESS TOWARD CHILDREN

Something to cherish:

But when the goodness and loving kindness of God our Savior appeared, he saved us, not because of works done by us in righteousness, but according to his own mercy, by the washing of regeneration and renewal of the Holy Spirit, whom he poured out on us richly through Jesus Christ our Savior, so that being justified by his grace we might become heirs according to the hope of eternal life. —Titus 3:4–7

Something to sing:

"All the Way My Savior Leads Me" by Chris Tomlin and Matt Redman

Something to read:

Boundaries with Kids: How Healthy Choices Grow Healthy Children by Dr. Henry Cloud and Dr. John Townsend

Something to consider:

- Where have I been unkind, demanding, and distracted? What is one way I could be kind today instead?

- Am I serving my child out of obligation or compulsion? How can I create a wise boundary and serve my child cheerfully, compelled by God's love for me?

- How is God lavishing me with kindness now? "My cup overflows" (Ps. 23:5). What would it look like for God's kindness to spill over to others?

MY PRAYER FOR YOU: *May you see God's kindness in the face of Christ, and may it melt your heart. May God give you good ideas to teach your child kindness every day. And may He invigorate you to be the hands and feet of Christ in your home and abroad.*

Chapter 11

AN APPETITE FOR GOODNESS

Oh, taste and see that the LORD is good!

—PSALM 34:8

EXPECT GOD TO SATISFY YOU
WITH GOODNESS, TRUTH, AND BEAUTY

Twenty years from now, when my children are adults, would you ask them what they loved best about childhood? I'm sure their answers will vary—from chickens to trampolines to picture books—but I hope at least one of them will say, "Morning Time." For as long as I can remember, I've carved out a special time on weekday mornings to gather the children together to think about things that are particularly good, true, and beautiful.

Over the years, we've memorized hymns, poems, and passages of Scripture together. We've prayed and talked about God. We've laughed and cried over books like *Charlotte's Web* and *Homer Price*. We've admired masterpieces and created some of our own. And—over and over—we've recited the names of the months, the days of the week, and the years passing by.

Part of my educational philosophy (yep, I have one) aligns with this observation often attributed to the ancient Greek philosopher Plutarch: "The mind is not a vessel to be filled, but a fire to be kindled." I work hard to make sure Morning Time isn't simply a recitation of facts, but instead a kindling of the inner flame to develop strong, curious minds and compassionate hearts. I often ask the Holy Spirit to work through Morning Time to build a relationship with each child and make our work fruitful and lasting. Sometimes Morning Time looks exactly as I had hoped, but not often. Nonetheless, I've been at it for many years, and I hope to stick with it because even on the distracted, rambunctious, or weary days, meditating on the goodness of God does wonders for us.

THE CANDLELIT MORNING TIME

One of my favorite Morning Times happened during a short-lived season in which we met together over candlelight. I had come across an inspiring photograph of some children watercolor painting at a table scattered with beeswax candles. It looked so lovely, I had to try it. I placed two white candlesticks in the middle of our kitchen table hoping the candlelight would help Morning Time feel memorable and set apart from the rest of the day. I guess you could say my wish came true: candlelight did set Morning Time apart, for one day anyway.

That day, the candles were casting a warm glow around the room while the kids read a poem aloud together. Suddenly, an odd smell wafted through the air. My ever-observant nine-year-old daughter gasped and pointed at her brother, whispering, "His hair is on fire." Sure enough, her little brother was kneeling on his chair, leaning over his book, sounding out a particularly difficult word while—unbeknownst to him—a tuft of his hair smoldered in the candle's flame. Startled by our sudden silence, he looked up with raised eyebrows as if to ask, "Is something wrong?" Meanwhile, a thin trail of smoke ascended from his head. I jumped into action and dampened the flame before it could do any harm.

Thankfully, he wasn't any worse for the wear. I snuffed out the candles and we settled down to a less hazardous (albeit less romantic) Morning Time. We launched into the hymn of the week, but all I could think about was my son's perplexed little face and the thin trail of

I burst out laughing until tears rolled down my face. The kids laughed, too, because uncanny things happen when earthbound humans feast on the things of God.

smoke ascending from the top of his head. I thought about how, over the years, I've tried just about everything to kindle a fire in my children's minds—sometimes successfully, other times not so much—and how I've longed for the Holy Spirit to be with us in those times, but I never imagined something so similar to Pentecost itself.

A smile broke out across my face and then I burst out laughing until tears rolled down my face. The kids threw their heads back and laughed, too, because uncanny things happen when earthbound humans feast on the things of God—sometimes we are uplifted, sometimes comforted, and other times, we are downright entertained.

A big part of my motherhood journey has been about tasting the goodness of God and sharing it with my children. Morning Time is just one part of the day in which we feast on His goodness together. Mothers have a unique opportunity to discover God's goodness and share it with our kids.

WHAT GOODNESS IS

In order to nurture our children with goodness, we need to know what "goodness" means. Although we use the word "good" in many different contexts, God owns the word. From the beginning of Scripture to the end, God shows Himself to be good, to do good, and to make good things. When God created the light, He said, "It is good," and when He created male and female, He said, "It is very good." Then, in the book of Revelation at the end of Scripture, we read about God's plan to renew the earth and dwell with people face-to-face, and it is *good*.

The entire cosmos is wrapped up in an epic battle between good and evil. God is on the side of good and we are, by birth, on the side of evil. As His enemies, we are entirely devoid of goodness and have no hope of conjuring it up by ourselves, but we do find hope in this:

> *When the goodness and loving kindness of God our Savior appeared, he saved us, not because of works done by us in righteousness, but according to his own mercy.*—Titus 3:4–5

Jesus is the source and expression of God's goodness: He is the wellspring from whom goodness overflows into our lives, changing us from people who used to live for ourselves into people who now live for God. We now live as citizens of His good kingdom: we think the thoughts of Christ, speak the truth in love, and look through grace-filled eyes. We discover God's goodness in the gospel and in creation, from raspberries to solar systems. Our once black-and-white lives burst into full color. We see God's goodness invading our broken world. We hear His invitation to bask in every good gift and to worship Him for it. Day in and day out, you and I are proclaiming one resounding message to our children: "God is good!"

WHAT GOODNESS DOES

If a child's mind is like a fire to be ignited, then his soul is like a deep well to be filled. What we pour into our child's soul matters greatly. Consider these Scriptures emphasizing the importance—and impact—of feeding our children on the goodness of God:

> *Psalm 78:4–7:*
> *We will not hide them from their children,*
> *but tell to the coming generation*
> *the glorious deeds of the Lord, and his might,*
> *and the wonders that he has done. . . .*
> *which he commanded our fathers*
> *to teach to their children,*
> *that the next generation might know them,*
> *the children yet unborn,*
> *and arise and tell them to their children,*
> *so that they should set their hope in God*
> *and not forget the works of God,*
> *but keep his commandments.*

> *Proverbs 4:23 NIV:*
> *Above all else, guard your heart,*
> *for everything you do flows from it.*

> *Proverbs 22:6:*
> *Train up a child in the way he should go;*
> *even when he is old he will not depart from it.*

> *Galatians 6:9–10:*
> *Let us not grow weary of doing good, for in due season we will reap, if we do not give up. So then, as we have opportunity, let*

us do good to everyone, and especially to those who are of the household of faith.

GOODNESS AND BUSYNESS

I must confess, I get swept up in the busyness of everyday life and breeze by the goodness of God as if my life didn't depend upon it. Thankfully, this doesn't deter God from spreading a feast before me and welcoming me to sit down and eat.

In Deuteronomy 6, God calls us to teach His goodness to our children, but He also—and first—calls us to make sure His goodness is in *our* hearts. To show you what I mean, I've highlighted the word *you* in part of Deuteronomy 6 as God addresses mothers and fathers. As you read it, I hope you can see how much God cares about your appetite for goodness and how it will fuel your life.

We all need what is good: Christ-centered worship, fresh air, beauty, truth, exercise, music, literature, adventure, tradition, celebration, service, fun, and friendship.

*[**You**] hear therefore, O Israel, and [**you**] be careful to do [God's commands], that it may go well with **you**, and that **you** may multiply greatly, as the LORD, the God of **your** fathers, has promised **you**, in a land flowing with milk and honey. [**You**] [h]ear, O Israel: The LORD our God, the LORD is one. **You** shall love the LORD **your** God with all **your** heart*

*and with all **your** soul and with all **your** might. And these
words that I command **you** today shall be on **your** heart. **You**
shall teach them diligently to **your** children, and shall talk of
them when **you** sit in **your** house, and when **you** walk by the
way, and when **you** lie down, and when **you** rise. **You** shall
bind them as a sign on **your** hand, and they shall be as frontlets
between **your** eyes. **You** shall write them on the doorposts of
your house and on **your** gates.—Deuteronomy 6:3–9*

God has prepared a table before you where you can feast on His
goodness every day. You'll discover it all around: through food,
fresh air, exercise, music, art, science, literature, adventure, tradition, celebration, service, fun, and friendship. Once you have
tasted the goodness of the Lord, you'll want more and you'll
want to share it with your child, saying, "Oh, taste and see that the
LORD is good!" (Ps. 34:8). What a blessing it is to be a mother
and to share goodness with our kids. Let's hold good things in
our minds, fill our time with good works, and teach our children
about the glory of God in His Word and in the world He has made.

*Surely goodness and mercy shall follow me all the days of my
life: and I will dwell in the house of the LORD for ever.*
—Psalm 23:6 KJV

When it comes to pursuing goodness for my children and
for myself, it helps me to think like a museum curator or a sharp-
eyed gatekeeper. We moms have this amazing opportunity to

welcome truth, goodness, and beauty into our homes and send unhealthy and unholy things on their way. It's powerful! It's life-changing! And it's a lifelong endeavor that must be textured with plenty of grace and wisdom. Our understanding of "What is good?" develops as we walk with Jesus and learn more about what it takes for a child (and a mama) to thrive. Here are some ideas for exercising this aspect of your awesome calling:

Surround yourself with other people—especially older women—who are further down the road than you are. What are their homes like? How do they spend their time? What do they talk about? What media do they consume? What books do they read? Keep your eye open for what it takes to become a woman of God. Learn what it takes to nurture a child and build a home.

Every so often, take time to go through your home and consider your books, music, artwork, and media. Do they reflect God's good heart for humanity? Without being legalistic, make some proactive choices to get rid of anything that isn't beneficial. Accentuate and cherish the things in your home that are good!

Then—here's the fun part—make a plan to fill your home with good things that will nourish each member of your family. Take it slow and steady. And remember, a little goes a long way.

Take a good look at your calendar. Do you fill your days with life-giving work, play, experiences, and relationships? Do you take time to appreciate God's gifts in everyday life? Schedule it in! Write it on your calendar and you'll be much more likely to do it.

Every time you pray with your child, get in the habit of thanking

God for one specific thing, whether that is a warm shower, your baby's giggle, or a song you heard on your way to the store. Thank Him for the big things too, like a resolved conflict, a granted prayer request, or an opportunity to be kind.

When you notice God's goodness in the Bible, mark it with a certain color ink or a special symbol like an asterisk. Share your discovery with a friend.

Begin each day by anticipating one of God's good gifts to you: "Today, I am excited to savor _____."

At the end of each day write, "Today, I saw the goodness of God. Here's how: _____."

•   •   •

I'm thinking again about my son whose hair smoldered in the candle's flame. This past year, he and I have been sitting down to read the Bible together, one chapter at a time. Along the way, we've faced obstacles: we've been interrupted and discouraged. In fact, one day, when everything seemed determined to prevent us from reading the Bible, I literally leaned over like a defensive linebacker and pushed my way to the dining room table where he was waiting for me. By sticking with it, we've read several books of the Bible together. To be honest, sometimes I wonder if either of us is gaining much from the habit. But then, there are days like the one when we read John 19:26–27. Something special happened when my son was reading aloud about Jesus being on the cross and he got to this part:

When Jesus saw his mother and the disciple whom he loved standing nearby, he said to his mother, "Woman, behold your son!" Then he said to the disciple, "Behold, your mother!" And from that hour the disciple took her to his own home.

My son looked up at me with shining eyes and whispered, "Oh, wow." For there was Jesus, showing us His good heart and His matchless love for His mother and His friend, inviting them to care for each other. There was Jesus, inviting each of us to care for one another on His behalf. I saw a fire kindled in my son's mind and a deep well filled in his soul. He tasted the goodness of the Lord that day. And so did I.

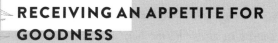

RECEIVING AN APPETITE FOR GOODNESS

Something to cherish:

Whatever is true, whatever is honorable, whatever is just, whatever is pure, whatever is lovely, whatever is commendable, if there is any excellence, if there is anything worthy of praise, think about these things. What you have learned and received and heard and seen in me—practice these things, and the God of peace will be with you.—Philippians 4:8–9

Something to sing:

"I Get to Be the One" by JJ Heller

Something to read:

The Lifegiving Home by Sally and Sarah Clarkson

Something to consider:

- Am I ingesting the goodness of God on a regular basis? If not, God, will You help me do that?

- How may I share God's goodness with my children today?

- Heavenly Father, will You give me a friend in this journey to share good ideas, books, plans, and more as we give goodness to our kids?

MY PRAYER FOR YOU: *Whenever you receive good gifts—from forgiveness and grace to sunrises and snuggles—may you remember that they come from your heavenly Father. May you learn how to fill your heart and home with life-giving words, things, and experiences. And may you and your child develop hearty appetites for goodness, causing you to draw near to the source of all goodness, God Himself.*

Chapter 12

FAITHFULNESS IN SMALL THINGS

Your faith—more precious than gold.

—1 PETER 1:7

EXPECT TO GET TO THE END OF EVERY DAY AND SAY, "GOD WAS FAITHFUL TO ME TODAY"

He was only four years old when he courageously grabbed the chest of gold and escaped the pirate ship. His wide eyes darted to and fro as he scouted out a place to hide. Several pirates clung to the ship while others leapt into the air in hot pursuit of our brave hero. The summer afternoon rang with loud shouts and explosive cannon shots.

Any onlooker would have seen a slew of children climbing on a swing set and chasing each other around the backyard, but these nine pirates—my six children and a friend's three sons—saw themselves clambering aboard a creaky old vessel in the middle of the South Seas and fighting for their lives over lost treasure. It was a classic childhood day I won't forget anytime soon. I took some photos, knowing my friend would want to see her adorable boys completely immersed in their epic battle.

While her sons ate popcorn and played pirates at our house, my friend lay in her bed at home enduring hyperemesis gravidarum, a serious and debilitating condition of excessive vomiting during pregnancy. Usually spunky and enthused about motherhood, this beautiful woman was seven weeks pregnant and already feeling weak and weary. Some days, she would start throwing up even if she opened her mouth to speak. She parented from the couch, lights dim, doing the best she could. One day, when she had a few moments of relief from the nausea, she sent me a tearful video message. "I feel so sad," she said. "I wanted this school year to be special, but most days I send the boys outside or downstairs to play by themselves. I can't be the mom I want to be. I'm so discouraged."

My heart went out to her and I sent her a message saying so. I have never suffered from that malady, but I have known the agony of weakness in motherhood, and it is terrible. I'm sure you know it, too: when you simply cannot engage with or provide for your child the way you want to.

SERIOUS TROUBLES

My friend's desperation brought to my mind the months after I had given birth to our fourth baby and plunged into postpartum depression. At my postpartum appointment, the doctor asked if I was feeling "blue," which I wasn't, so I didn't tell her about my uncharacteristic paranoia. I didn't tell her about the vivid gruesome thoughts that bombarded my mind day after day. (I wish now that I had said something and received medical help. If you are struggling with abnormal thoughts or depression after pregnancy, please consult your caregiver.) I assumed postpartum depression felt like a melancholy drama; now I know that it can also feel like a horror film. It took me a long time to tell anyone about my struggles because I didn't know what would happen if I opened my mouth to speak. *What would people think? Would they take my kids away?* The illogical—but very real—battle in my mind was unrelenting and isolating.

The same God who was with me in this moment with this troubling thought would be with me in future moments, too, with future fears, no matter what. He is a step-by-step kind of Shepherd.

I was so preoccupied with my fearful thoughts that I forgot to interact with my baby. I knew it was important for her to hear my voice, so I stuck handwritten notes on the wall, telling myself what to say when I couldn't get out of my own head. In the mornings, I could barely open the nursery door for fear of what I might discover inside. Every day was a battle. I _gled to care for my children and keep up with life in general. I wasn't the mom I wanted to be.

In time, I told my husband what was going on. He did whatever it took to get me more sleep, more help, and more time with friends. With a little research, he discovered a possible cause of my paranoia: the negative effects of reading from a lighted screen during nighttime feedings. I turned my screen off and kept the nursery lights low. With a couple of practical changes, I experienced quick relief. But the most significant change occurred when the Lord taught me to trust Him with my intrusive thoughts.

I put a note from 1 Peter 5:7 on the nursery door that said, "Cast all your anxieties on him, because he cares for you." Instead of trying harder not to think about terrifying things, I learned to talk openly with God and thank Him that my fears weren't coming to pass at that moment. Gradually, I learned that the same God who is with me in *this* moment with *this* troubling thought will be with me in future moments, too, with future fears, no matter what. He is a step-by-step kind of Shepherd. God's faithful companionship got me through a very difficult season of motherhood.

Over the years, I've walked with many friends through postpartum depression. The weeks, months, and sometimes years following birth or adoption can be both beautiful and dark. I'm convinced that whenever a woman is caring for a new child, she is wise to seek and accept help from other people. God works wonders through husbands, friends, mentors, and medical professionals. God cares for us while we are caring for our babies, and this can take many different forms from a good night's sleep to much-needed medical intervention.

My friend's struggle with hyperemesis gravidarum also made me think of a time—not too long ago—when I was up all night with a head cold, propped up on pillows, breathing through my mouth like Napoleon Dynamite. At dawn, my sinuses finally decided to drain. Now that I was finally able to inhale air through my nostrils, I thought maybe, just maybe, I could sleep. I pulled the covers over my head to try. Just then, something important came to mind: *Your kids will be up any minute now.* I sighed and looked out of the window. The black of night was giving way to a luscious shade of gray. Thick, low-lying clouds obstructed my view of the mountains in the distance. In time, the wind would blow the storm clouds away and I'd be able to see the mountains again.

This reminded me of God, who remains faithful even when our health, circumstances, or feelings cloud our vision. Challenging circumstances will blow away like storm clouds revealing that God was with us all along. But for the moment, my head throbbed and my body ached. I could hear the kids waking up with hunger and bathroom needs. Ryan was already on his way to a big day at work, so I had no other choice. I had to be a mom today, to love my children, nurture them, pray for them, teach them the ways of God, and point them to Jesus. I wanted to be faithful, but it felt impossible.

STEEP MOUNTAINS AND HOLY HILLS

That day loomed before me like a steep mountain and I wondered how I would ever make it to bedtime. Have you had a day—or days or a season—when it seemed there was a mountain looming before you? Have you ever wondered how you'll make it to bedtime? Whether you are suffering from a debilitating pregnancy, postpartum depression, or any other tough circumstances, the words of Scripture ring true: the Lord will be strong when you are weak (2 Cor. 12:9).

Psalm 121 is a great help and is written out for you below. The Lord will not tire of your needs, and He isn't turned off by your struggles. He will be your ever-present help around the clock. Who is more faithful than Jesus, who has seen humanity through the fall, left His throne to come to earth, died on the cross, and rose again for you? Who is more faithful than the One whose eyes are on you, who knows the number of hairs on your head, and discerns your thoughts from afar? No one is more faithful than the Lord who will "keep you forevermore."

> *I lift up my eyes to the hills.*
> *From where does my help come?*
> *My help comes from the LORD,*
> *who made heaven and earth.*
> *He will not let your foot be moved;*
> *he who keeps you will not slumber.*
> *Behold, he who keeps Israel*
> *will neither slumber nor sleep.*

The LORD is your keeper;
   the LORD is your shade on your right hand.
The sun shall not strike you by day,
   nor the moon by night.
The LORD will keep you from all evil;
   he will keep your life.
The LORD will keep
   your going out and your coming in
   from this time forth and forevermore.

GOLD IN EVERY SEASON

Seasons change dramatically in Pennsylvania. Winter spreads a blanket of snow over the bare trees until a warm breeze coaxes new buds from the branches. The summer sun finds us picnicking under green leafy canopies until a sudden cold snap sends us scrambling for our sweaters as crimson leaves glide down to the earth. Motherhood, too, changes dramatically, giving way to its own seasons of rest, growth, and harvest. While we adapt to our constantly changing lives as moms, we can rely on God's constancy. One of my favorite hymns, "Great Is Thy Faithfulness" by Thomas Chisholm, expresses His steadfastness perfectly. If you're not familiar with this one, I invite you to look up the words or listen to it being sung. Oh, it's so good!

In seasons of dormancy when we are lying on the couch in a dimly lit room, God is still at work. We might not be able to do much, but we can look for His faithfulness and be amazed by His unfaltering care for us. We may worry about our children: *Are they getting enough attention? Is our weakness dragging them down?*

But God works through our difficult seasons to draw our children close to Himself and to plant good seeds in their souls. Our children learn a lot from us when we are weak. They see other Christians visit and care for us. They learn life skills like how to suffer, recover, and rely on the Lord. They meet a God who will never leave or forsake them (Heb. 13:5).

If your child can say, "God was faithful to my mom when she was sick or injured or depressed," God gave your child gold in a season when you thought he or she was missing out. Often in our weakest seasons, our children take their first steps in our Good Shepherd's footprints: they glimpse His faithfulness and learn to be like Him.

> *Mothering is not like pouring water through a sieve where each day's investment runs out by nightfall. Mothering is like planting and cultivating seeds in the rich soil of our children's souls.*

Thankfully, motherhood probably won't be a never-ending winter. At just the right time, some light will warm the soil of our souls and we'll feel more like ourselves again. When we are well rested, healthy, and clearheaded, we'll want to seek the Lord's guidance for how we can make the most of our time with our kids. Using all that we learned when we were down and out, the Holy Spirit will grow the fruit of faithfulness in us and help us stick with our kids no matter what, keep our word, and do what's right.

Remember, mothering is not like pouring water through a sieve where each day's investment runs out by nightfall, but instead, mothering is like filling a deep well. Each day's work accumulates a faith in God, a Jesus-centered worldview, and a Christlike character that will sustain our children even when we are weak. Becoming wise about the seasons of motherhood means seeking God's grace to do our best when we are able, trusting Him with the outcome.

• • •

In preparation for writing this chapter, I asked my children, "When am I a faithful mom?" I assumed their answers would be along the lines of "When you keep your word, take care of us, stick with us, and make meals." But their answers were different than I expected. They said I'm a faithful mom when I thank God that He provides food for us. They talked about the times when I've celebrated because God provided winter coats or helped us find a lost toddler sock. They said I'm a faithful mom when I tell them that God reminded me of something from His Word at just the right time, or when I tell them that He can handle their questions and doubts. My kids weren't describing *my* faithfulness at all: they were describing God's. All I need to do is notice it and share it with them.

• • •

I want to tell you the next part of the story about my friend who lay on the couch, too sick to speak. She endured intense sickness well into her second trimester. Just when she was beginning to feel better, she discovered that her precious baby girl had gone to be with the Lord. Like Juliette, Annie Margaret was stillborn. The loss was devastating. Friends and family gathered together to cry, sing, and remember God's promises together.

When I originally wrote this chapter, I didn't know that my friend's pregnancy would end in tragedy. In fact, I drafted a conclusion about a happy birth, saying that my friend's suffering paid off because now she had her baby and she felt better and it was all worth it. But life rarely goes according to our plans. My friend doesn't know why she was so sick for a pregnancy that ended in stillbirth. She doesn't know why her sons had to go weeks without their regular energetic momma. All she can say is that she looked for God's faithfulness each devastating day and found it. God carried her through a season of motherhood that otherwise would have been unbearable. He carried her baby girl and her fearsome pirate boys too. He was faithful to each one of them and will be forever. I believe they came out of that difficult season with hearts full of gold.

RECEIVING FAITHFULNESS IN SMALL THINGS

Something to cherish:
It is good to give thanks to the LORD, to sing praises to your name, O Most High; to declare your steadfast love in the morning, and your faithfulness by night. —Psalm 92:1–2

Something to sing:
"He's Always Been Faithful" by Sara Groves

Something to read:
Risen Motherhood: Gospel Hope for Everyday Moments by Emily Jensen and Laura Wifler

Something to consider:

- How has God been faithful to me today in big and small ways?

- What is one thing I can tell my child about God's specific acts of faithfulness today?

- Which habit can I develop, one step at a time, to grow in faithfulness?

MY PRAYER FOR YOU: *May each season of motherhood be marked indelibly by God's unchanging faithfulness, growing your faith in Him. May you become more and more faithful as you raise your child in all sorts of circumstances, having wisdom to work and rest, sow and reap, in the appropriate seasons.*

Chapter 13

LIFE-SUSTAINING GENTLENESS

*Be not angry that you cannot make others
as you wish them to be, since you cannot
make yourself as you wish to be.*[18]

—THOMAS À KEMPIS

EXPECT JESUS TO BE IN THE MESS WITH YOU

As I began writing this chapter on gentleness, two stories vied for my attention. They both involve bodily fluids. (Did you expect to get through a book about motherhood without a healthy dose of bodily fluids? Impossible.) The first story happened one morning in early November when I pulled into the parking lot for a women's Bible study. Seasons of motherhood haven't always allowed for me to attend a Bible study, but I've joined whenever my kids' ages and stages made it feasible.

Nonetheless, getting out the door by 8:30 in the morning with three small children and an infant was no small thing. I had nursed the baby, fed the kids a reasonable breakfast, remembered my Bible study materials, and made the trek through country roads with minimal drama. We arrived at 9:00 on the dot. Amazing. I would be on time for the first time in ages. I swung the van door open and began unhooking and unclicking the kids from their car seats. When I scooped the baby up from her car seat, my fingers oozed through a warm creamy substance smeared across her back. Horrified, I turned her around and saw the telltale signs of an epic blow-out diaper.

Blow-out diapers are always a disaster, but even more so away from home. No amount of emergency training helps when you are suddenly holding a poop-covered baby. Significant, existential questions come to mind like, *What in the world should I do now?* I put the baby back into the goopy car seat and with the tippy top of one clean pinky finger, I grabbed the handle of the diaper bag. I'll leave the rest to your imagination, but somehow, I got the whole mess—wipes, diaper, onesie, sleeper, socks, and all—into a plastic bag destined for the garbage.

THOSE EPIC MOMENTS

I put a clean diaper on the baby and rummaged in the diaper bag for a fresh onesie and sleeper. I didn't have to rummage long before I remembered that she had needed those spare clothes two days earlier and I hadn't restocked the diaper bag. I searched the van for something to protect her from the chilly November air. I found it shoved in the glove compartment: a blue Ocean City, Maryland, T-shirt with a cartoon crab on the front saying, "Sometimes crabby but always cute." Size 2T. It would have to do.

I tucked the baby inside my coat, ushered the kids into the building, and opened the door to the nursery. We were twenty minutes late. The childcare workers welcomed the big kids and busied them with friends and toys. A grandmotherly volunteer sat in a rocking chair eagerly waiting for a baby to snuggle. I sighed and handed my daughter to her. She raised her eyebrows at the baggy blue T-shirt and little bare legs. "I'm sorry," I said as if I were in sixth grade and had forgotten my homework. "She just had a blow-out diaper, and this is the only thing I have for her to wear."

The woman surprised me with a direct, "This is not okay. You're the mom. You should always have a warm change of clothes for her." I knew she meant well. She was in mama-bear mode and didn't know how her words stung. I decided to receive her words with a smile because God knows I've been insensitive toward other mothers too. Besides, two things were certain: one, she would snuggle my baby with extra warmth that day, and two, when I got home, I would restock our diaper bag so thoroughly that we could go to the moon and back without a hitch.

I was standing in the front of the room, expressing these thoughts aloud, when, suddenly . . .

The other story happened five years later, when baby #6 was a newborn. By now, my older kids were able to do their schoolwork independently, so I did what any reasonable homeschooling woman with six children—including a newborn and a two-year-old—would do. I didn't just sign up for the study and hope to attend, probably arriving twenty minutes late with a baby in an oversized T-shirt. Instead, I said, "Are you looking for a consistent, reliable leader? Here I am!"

On the first day of the study, I miraculously nursed the baby, fed the kids breakfast, packed the diaper bag, assigned the schoolwork, and got all seven of us to the church on time. When we arrived, my baby seemed fussy, so I wore her in an Ergo and bobbed up and down as I invited the ladies to grab their coffee and take their seats. My face beamed with joy to see these women who were gathering to study God's Word together.

I was standing in the front of the room, sharing opening remarks when, suddenly, my sweet baby began projectile vomiting. If you've ever experienced a baby's projectile vomiting, you know three things: one, it's terrifying; two, it seems to last forever; and three, it produces humanly impossible amounts of fluid. I stopped midsentence as what seemed like a gallon of warm milk poured all over me. When the vomiting stopped, my baby sighed, snuggled in, and fell asleep, but both of us were drenched from head to toe. A friend took over the meeting so I could waddle out of the room, straight legged. I didn't know how to begin cleaning up the mess. Three women grabbed paper towels from the bathroom and surrounded me. I stood in the hallway, my arms out to the side, while they gently wiped my hair, patted the baby carrier, and pressed wads of paper towels against my jeans to soak up the milk. I'll never forget the woman who knelt down and carefully wiped my black flats. Tears of gratitude rolled down my cheeks. They said it was no big deal and they had been in my position before.

THOSE BASIC NEEDS

Blow-out diapers and projectile vomiting are just the beginning of a mother's relationship with bodily fluids. Over my years of mothering, I've visited more bathrooms in T.J. Maxx, McDonald's, and grungy gas stations than I would like to admit. I've performed modern-day miracles in porta-potties with a preschooler in one arm and a baby in an Ergo, while trying to not touch *anything*. My favorite public bathroom is in a quaint restaurant on our way to Grandmom and Grandpop's house. The bathrooms are for customers only, so if we stop there, I have to buy a piece of pie. Motherhood doesn't come with many nonnegotiable treats, so to be forced to enjoy a piece of pie every now and then works for me. The lemon meringue is exquisite.

Speaking of bathrooms, a friend recently asked me to share my potty-training insights. To be honest, I don't have much to share. Although everyone in our family is potty-trained, I'm not quite sure how it happened. We used the same approach every time, but each child responded differently. One of our kiddos took longer than the others, one was too distracted to care, one relapsed after two years of consistency, one developed a slight neurosis about potty germs, and one amazing child figured it out within twenty-four hours and announced, "I'm potty-trained, Mom." In my experience, there is no formula for fail-safe, accident-free potty training, but I have learned two principles that have helped along the way: *treat your child with dignity* and *prepare for accidents*.

Dignity: Something about the inconvenience, mess, and general grossness of bathroom needs can bring out the worst in me. My friend Jenny, a mom of eight, gave me great advice: "Treat your child the way you want to be treated when they help *you* go to the potty someday." This has become my golden rule of potty training and it shapes the way I respond to my child's most basic needs. All I do is take a minute to imagine the way I want my children to treat me when I am old and helpless, and I know exactly how I want to treat them.

Accidents: I learned the second principle from my friend Renee who listened patiently as I ranted about one of my kiddos still having occasional accidents two years into the potty-training process. Renee nodded along and said, "I plan on my kids having accidents until they are four or five years old. I keep a change of clothes in the car and try not to make a big deal about it." This mentality was a game changer for me. Being prepared for accidents helps me to extend grace to my child as well as to myself. I'm not shocked or angry. We just clean it up and move on.

JESUS IS GENTLY IN THE MESS WITH YOU

God works through the inconvenient, messy, even gross aspects of motherhood to give us the gift of gentleness. Nothing else in motherhood so poignantly illustrates Jesus' heart toward us. Jesus is for messy and inconvenient people. When Jesus dwelled on earth, He touched unlovely people in their most humiliating moments. He embraced a leprous man, befriended an adulterous woman, and washed His disciples' feet. He ate with sinners, defended the lowly, and blessed the outcasts.

Jesus was even gentle when soldiers arrested Him in the garden of Gethsemane. When Peter cut off Malchus's ear, Jesus told Peter, "Put your sword back into its place," and then He touched Malchus and healed him (Matt. 26:52). When people slapped Him in face, beat Him on the back, and demanded a response, Jesus became like a lamb, quiet and meek. While He was being crucified, He prayed, "Father, forgive them, for they know not what they do" (Luke

Jesus doesn't expect us to get our act together. Instead, He enters our mess.

23:34). As He suffered on the cross, Jesus was meeting us in our mess, removing our filthy sin, and clothing us in His spotless righteousness.

Still today, Jesus welcomes people who "labor and are heavy laden"—like you and me—to come to Him because He is "gentle and lowly in heart" (Matt. 11:28–29). He wants to touch us and speak to us with life-giving gentleness. Our spiritual needs aren't much different from our children's physical needs: every day, we make a mess of things and can't comprehend how our sin offends God, hurts ourselves, and affects other people. Yet every day, Jesus kneels and cleans up our mess for us. He cups our faces in His hands and says, "I gave up My throne in glory to be with you in your worst moment. Redeeming you matters more to Me than anything else in the universe." Jesus doesn't expect us to get our act together or to punish ourselves for our inadequacies. Instead, He enters our mess, treats us with dignity, and is prepared to rescue us at any time.

GENTLY ENTERING THE MESS
WITH YOUR CHILD

Just as we can learn to respond gently to a child's physical needs, we can learn to respond gently to a child's spiritual needs as well. Unlike potty accidents, children never outgrow their need for a Savior. We'll want to be careful as we come alongside our kids in their spiritual brokenness: the same potty-training principles of treating them with dignity and being prepared for accidents apply. It might also help to think about what we do when we clean up a broken dish or a shattered light bulb. We pay attention. We keep our eyes open. We step lightly and try not to make more of a mess or cause more

Being gentle may seem a bit risky at first, but once we get the hang of it, we'll see gentleness for what it is: Triumphant. Unassailable.

injury. This is the type of care we want to use when we are addressing a child's sin.

The apostle Paul often encourages us to be gentle with one another. These two excerpts from his letters are particularly helpful as we consider our opportunity to grow in Christlike gentleness toward our children:

> *If anyone is caught in any transgression, you who are spiritual should restore him in a spirit of gentleness. Keep watch on yourself, lest you too be tempted. Bear one another's burdens, and so fulfill the law of Christ.*—Galatians 6:1–2

> *The Lord's servant must not be quarrelsome but kind to everyone, able to teach, patiently enduring evil, correcting his opponents with gentleness. God may perhaps grant them repentance leading to a knowledge of the truth.*
> —2 Timothy 2:24–25

In light of this, I've brainstormed some tangible ways you and I can respond gently to our children's sin. What would you add to the list?

- We can listen.
- We can pray.
- We can wait on the Lord to work in their hearts.
- We can correct them when they are wrong.
- We can remind them about the grace of God through Jesus, lavished on all repentant sinners.

- We can say we are with them and for them, no matter what.
- We can say, "I forgive you."
- We can teach them to get back up and say, "I can learn from that."
- We can offer specific Scriptures and practical assistance to strengthen them against temptation.
- We can empathize when they experience the consequences of sin.
- We can share our own stories and God's faithfulness, when appropriate.
- We can rejoice when they experience victory over sin.
- We can smile at them and look them in the eye.
- We can pull them into a hug, rub their back, or sit by their side.
- We can tell them we've been there too.

Being gentle may seem a bit risky at first—we may be taken advantage of—but once we get the hang of it, I think we'll see gentleness for what it is: Triumphant. Unassailable. The very heart of Christ. In a world that advocates self-preservation, punishment for wrongdoing, and cruelty toward people who are weak, we are invited to extend the life-giving power of gentleness.

RECEIVING LIFE-SUSTAINING GENTLENESS

Something to cherish:

Come to me, all who labor and are heavy laden, and I will give you rest. Take my yoke upon you, and learn from me, for I am gentle and lowly in heart, and you will find rest for your souls. For my yoke is easy, and my burden is light. —Matthew 11:28–30

Something to sing:

"I Want to Say I'm Sorry" by Andrew Peterson

Something to read:

Shepherding a Child's Heart by Tedd Tripp

Something to consider:

- Today, I want to confess my sin. Heavenly Father, please forgive me for_____. Thank You for treating me gently, forgiving me, and cleansing me from all unrighteousness.

- Today, I want to talk to You about my human weakness. I tend to make a mess of things whenever I _____. Thank You for treating me gently. Would You help me grow in this area?

- In what area does my child most need my gentleness today? How can I treat him or her gently?

MY PRAYER FOR YOU: *May you grasp the extent of your sin and wholeheartedly rely on Jesus to cleanse you from all unrighteousness. May the Holy Spirit teach you how to treat yourself and your child gently in all manner of circumstances. May you have wisdom to know how to come alongside your child in his or her spiritual brokenness, ever leaning on Jesus, our humble and gentle Savior.*

Chapter 14

SELF-CONTROL TO GO THE DISTANCE

*It is natural to quarrel, to be selfish,
to live a small-minded life. It is supernatural
to love unconditionally, to serve others,
to live a life of vision and faith.*

—SALLY CLARKSON[19]

EXPECT GOD TO STAY WITH YOU
THROUGH IT ALL

For several winters in a row, our whole family trekked out to
Ohio for a weeklong technology conference. While Ryan connected with people and ideas that helped him grow profession-
ally, our older kids attended classes on robotics, 3D printing, and

electronics. As if that weren't cool enough, the conference was also held at an indoor water park. In between classes, we bobbed in the wave pool and slipped down the waterslides.

My role was to support the troops. During the day, Ryan attended the conference while I took care of the kids. Every year, I wholeheartedly agreed to the arrangement, but I'll tell you what: it was not easy. It wasn't easy to feed a family of seven out of a mini microwave for a week, to keep track of five spunky kiddos in a water park as a giant bucket dumped water from the sky every three minutes, to dry bathing suits, help with showers, keep the peace, usher big kids to classes, and guide little kids from snacks to meltdowns to naps and back around again—all while making sure none of them pulled the fire alarm. Was it privileged? Yes. Full of happy memories? Perhaps. But was it easy? No.

DIAPER BAGS AND COMPUTER BAGS

Maybe that's why, one morning, as I was hauling an overstuffed diaper bag and lugging a double stroller through the conference center, I stopped in my tracks. My kids hopped around, excited to get to the waterslides, while I watched a group of women fill their coffee mugs at the complimentary coffee bar. They calmly placed their slim computer bags over their shoulders and headed off to their next session. There I stood in my sweatpants, hair in a messy bun, baby drool on my shoulder. I sighed as tears sprang to my eyes. I momentarily wished God had called me to do the work *they* were doing: earning a salary, networking with other professionals, and attending a conference. Instead, I was doling out snacks and folding pool towels. Maybe this wasn't God's best for me after all. I thought for sure I'd be further along by now.

This dilemma wasn't new to me. In fact, during that season of life, God was calling me to be a stay-at-home mom. On one hand, I thoroughly enjoyed the opportunity to invest my time in my kids, but on the other hand, I sometimes wondered if I should be pursuing a career instead. (I've long since learned that no matter what type of work God calls us to, we all wrestle with His playbook from time to time. In fact, a friend told me that although she would have been one of the women with a coffee mug and a computer bag, she would've been pining for a double stroller and a gaggle of kids at her side.)

At any rate, that day in the middle of the conference center, I knew God was calling me to keep my hand on the stroller. I knew He was calling me to stay the course. Would I obey? One thing was certain: if I was going to persist in this career-compromising, dream-altering, countercultural work, I needed help beyond myself. I needed God's gift of self-control.

A ROCKY RELATIONSHIP WITH SELF-CONTROL

To tell you the truth, self-control and I have had a rocky relationship dating back to second grade when my teacher handed me a brown 6 x 9 envelope with my report card tucked inside. Report

Card Day was usually a great day culminating in a celebratory dinner and a rare trip to the toy store. I pulled my report card out of the envelope, expecting good news. The teacher had evaluated me in character qualities like "Pays attention in class," and "Plays well with others." I was hoping for an array of plus signs indicating my strengths in each area, but this time a dark minus sign glared up at me. My heart sank. This was my first official failure. And it was in "self-control."

I was determined to make things right. I vowed to return the following year and work at self-control so that I would never receive a minus again. But when I lay in bed that night, I realized something important: even if I was able to earn all As and all plusses, I would still be wrestling with a sinful nature that I couldn't overcome on my own. I was so troubled by this evaluation that I woke my mom in the middle of the night to bare my soul. I leaned over her bed and whispered that I didn't want to do bad things, but I did them anyway, and when I wanted to do good things, I couldn't make myself do them. She got out of bed, took a Bible from the shelf, and sat next to me in the dimly lit hallway. She opened to the book of Romans where the apostle Paul expresses the same struggle. She read aloud,

> *For I do not understand my own actions. For I do not do what I want, but I do the very thing I hate. . . . I have the desire to do what is right, but not the ability to carry it out. . . . Wretched man that I am! Who will deliver me from this body of death? Thanks be to God through Jesus Christ our Lord!*
> *—Romans 7:15, 18, 24–25*

Even as a child, I knew something of Paul's agony. It comforted me to know I was not alone. This was likely the first time I felt the impact of my sinful nature and my need for Jesus. Suddenly, the truth that Jesus had set me free from sin became a tangible reality. Jesus had befriended me and welcomed me to live for Him— imperfectly, yes, but repentant, growing, and without condemnation. Over the years, I've discovered that Paul goes on to say that, in Christ, we are filled with the Holy Spirit. The solution to our ongoing battle against sin is to listen to the Holy Spirit and do what He says. As it turns out, self-control isn't just a wrestling match against impulsivity, and it isn't just self-discipline for self-discipline's sake. Rather, self-control is a wholehearted surrender to the Holy Spirit, to live as He deems best.

There is therefore now no condemnation for those who are in Christ Jesus. For the law of the Spirit of life has set you free in Christ Jesus from the law of sin and death.—Romans 8:1–2

As I sat next to my mom in the hallway marveling at these words for the first time, I couldn't have anticipated how they would comfort me years later when I had a crisis of faith in the middle of a tech conference. On that day, and many others like it when I face the temptation to abandon the work God has established for me, these words remind me that I am free to look beyond my selfish desires and to seek the Lord's will instead. If I'm reading Paul correctly, when a woman practices self-control and surrenders to Jesus—in whatever He is calling her to do—she maximizes her potential.

• • •

Fast-forward to one night not too long ago when I was sitting by my son's side reading *The Jesus Storybook Bible*. I instinctively put my hand over my heart when I read about Jesus' fierce determination to stay on the cross despite His body's desire to escape the pain. Deeply intrigued by this glimpse of Jesus' self-control on our behalf, I tucked my son in bed and opened my Bible to the same story. Before Jesus was arrested and crucified, He took His disciples to Gethsemane to pray. He needed time and space to surrender His personal desires to His heavenly Father and affirm that He would do His Father's will, no matter what the cost.

> **Soldiers nailed Jesus' hands and feet to the cross, but the nails didn't hold Him there: He held Himself there.**

We read in Matthew 26 how deeply sorrowful Jesus was at the prospect of the cross. He even prayed twice that He might not have to endure it, pleading for a way out, but ultimately surrendering— with all His heart—to His heavenly Father's will. Resolved to obey His Father, Jesus got up and turned His face toward His betrayer.

He could have appealed to His Father, who could have at once sent more than twelve legions of angels to rescue Him, but He didn't. Instead, He chose to be crucified to fulfill the Scriptures. Soldiers nailed Jesus' hands and feet to the cross, but the nails didn't hold Him there: He held Himself there. After centuries of heart-stirring promises, epic foreshadowing, show-stopping miracles, and wondrous prophecies, Jesus completed our redemption through one humble act of self-control.

SELF-CONTROL AND MOTHERHOOD

Even on our worst day, God looks at us and sees Christ's self-control. He hears Jesus' resolve, "Not as I will, but as you will." He sees Jesus set His face toward the cross and stay there in love. And then, the Holy Spirit moves in us so that we, too, may set our faces toward His will, and do it.

Self-control is the game changer in our walk of faith. It mobilizes every aspect of the fruit of the Spirit.

We tend to define "self-control" as the determination to do the ab workout or to not eat the cookie. Most of us hear the word "self-control" and immediately cringe with self-inflicted guilt about body image. But self-control is so much more than the secret to weight loss.

Self-control is *the* game changer in our walk of faith. It mobilizes every aspect of the fruit of the Spirit, making love, joy, peace, patience, kindness, goodness, faithfulness, and gentleness *happen* in us. Self-control is the grace-fueled, Holy Spirit–empowered grit to seek and do the will of God. It's the spiritual muscle to think the righteous thought, speak the righteous word, and do the righteous thing. Without self-control, Christlike virtues are only good ideas that never make their way into our actual lives.

Too often, my life is shaped by my emotions. I do what feels right in the moment. However, when I surrender to God, He helps me do what is right, no matter how I feel. Years ago, when our then-three-year-old son struggled to obey us, he would grasp himself by the shirt collar and turn himself in the right direction. We had never modeled this for him nor had we treated him this way ourselves, but we marveled at his natural demonstration of self-control. In a sense, this is what it looks like for you and me to obey too: through the power of the Holy Spirit, we grasp ourselves by the shirt collar and turn in the way we should go.

In Christ, we can rule over our emotions, make wise decisions, and overcome habits that we once thought we couldn't live without. He frees us to do His holy will. It is never easy—and it doesn't necessarily get easier over time—but it is always worthwhile; rather, it is always *wonderful*, far more wonderful than we can even imagine. In fact, if you are looking for the secret to a life well lived, look no further than the juicy, delicious, exhilarating fruit of self-control.

YOUR WELL-TENDED FIELD

Once when Jesus was talking about the cost of following Him, He said, "No one who puts his hand to the plow and looks back is fit for the kingdom of God" (Luke 9:62). This always makes me think about the farmer who plows our nearby fields. I'd love to know how many miles he puts on his tractor as he drives back and forth to plow, then fertilize, then plant, and finally harvest the same few acres of ground year after year. I wonder if he ever wants to leave the challenges of farm life and head to the beach for a well-earned vacation.

But when a farmer commits to feeding his family, livestock, and community, he keeps his hand to the plow, mile after mile, season after season. (Can you imagine how far he could travel if he logged those miles straight down the highway and not back and forth over the same plot of land?) At harvesttime, when the silos, wagons, wheelbarrows, freezers, and canning jars are stocked with good wholesome food, and when a plot of God's good earth has been lovingly

Whenever we want to run away or abandon His call, we'll need to remember that He will never leave us.

tended for yet another year, the farmer sees how very far he has traveled, and he's glad he stayed the course.

There I stood in the middle of the conference center, torn between God's calling to support my husband and kids for the week and my momentary desire for a different path. By God's grace, I gripped the handlebar, leaned my weight into the stroller, and wheeled it toward the room where Ryan was preparing to teach one of the Kids' Track sessions. If I hadn't stayed—if I hadn't surrendered to the will of God for me—I wouldn't have been standing in the back of the room with a squirmy toddler to hear my husband teach a room full of enthusiastic future techies about digital sound. I wouldn't have encouraged our children to help their daddy with his class. I wouldn't have seen our tween daughter's eyes light up about 3D printing, or high-fived our four-year-old when she slid down her first waterslide, or walked hand in hand with our toddler as he explored the baby pool.

My relationship with my husband and kids grew that week. God entered in when I least expected it—as I wrapped warm towels around my kids' shivering shoulders and served count-less bags of microwavable popcorn. To be with them and to help them thrive was a glimpse of how God must feel about being with us. And, surprisingly, even though I wasn't attending any thought-provoking sessions, except my husband's, or network-ing or having stimulating conversations over lunch, I grew, too: in character, maturity, and commitment. Mostly, I grew in awe of Jesus, who, given the choice between laying His life down for us or doing something else, picks us every time.

Whether God calls us to build a career, a ministry, a home, or all of the above; whether He asks us to carry a diaper bag, a computer bag, or a tool bag; whether He asks us to keep our hand to the stroller, the microphone, or the plow; whether He calls us to say the right thing, do the right thing, or think the right thing, we'll wrestle with obedience from time to time. We won't always see the benefit of doing things His way. We'll need His gift of self-control. And whenever we want to run away, we'll need to remember that He will never leave us and we'll lean on Him with our full weight.

For the record: any woman who is committed to loving God and people is never going to go as far as she thought she could go for herself. None of us will achieve self-actualization or maximize our potential. Not the way culture defines it, anyway. Let the tears fall because the truth of the matter is that when we say yes to God, we will go half the distance, but twice as far.

RECEIVING SELF-CONTROL TO GO THE DISTANCE

Something to cherish:
Now may the God of peace himself sanctify you completely, and may your whole spirit and soul and body be kept blameless at the coming of our Lord Jesus Christ. He who calls you is faithful; he will surely do it. —1 Thessalonians 5:23–24

Something to sing:
"Trust in You" by Lauren Daigle

Something to read:
Desperate: Hope for the Mom Who Needs to Breathe by Sarah Mae and Sally Clarkson

Something to consider:

- What encouragement can I find in Scripture regarding an area where I lack self-control?

- What personal desires do I need to surrender to God so that there is room for the Spirit's leading in my heart?

- What is God's will for me today? Is there something He would like to bring to my attention? May I respond to the Holy Spirit willingly.

MY PRAYER FOR YOU: *May you know the incomparable joy of surrendering your life to Jesus. When you are tempted to abandon His call in motherhood, may He give you the gift of self-control so that you may pray like Jesus, "Not My will, but Yours be done." May the Holy Spirit help you think the righteous thought, speak the righteous word, and do the righteous thing. And in every success and every failure, may you rest entirely in Christ, who held Himself to the cross—for you—until His work was accomplished.*

Chapter 15

COUNTLESS OPPORTUNITIES TO WORSHIP

Though the fig tree should not blossom,
nor fruit be on the vines . . .
yet I will rejoice in the LORD;
I will take joy in the God of my salvation.

—HABAKKUK 3:17–18

EXPECT TO WORSHIP GOD, EVEN WHEN YOU CANNOT SEE FRUIT

We've come to the final chapter, but certainly not to God's final gift to mothers. You and I will spend the rest of our lives discovering God's good gifts to moms. They'll rarely come individually wrapped but will grow in conjunction with other gifts: love and patience may grow side by side as you nurture a newborn. Goodness and faithfulness may blossom together as you raise a grade-schooler. An effective prayer life may grow alongside an ironclad trust in God as you walk alongside a teen. We'll want to keep our eyes open and our hearts warm to whatever God wants to give us next.

LOST FOOTING

Before we reach the final page, I want to share one more story that took place in our farmhouse on a Wednesday morning not too long ago. Our house smelled divine because, in a moment of domestic triumph, I had made pumpkin pancakes with homemade whipped cream. All six kids gathered around the kitchen table. They were so excited about this breakfast. The sunlight danced on their smiling faces as they helped set the table. We sat down and with bowed heads thanked God with grateful hearts. After the prayer, my five-year-old daughter picked up the glass bowl of whipped cream and skipped around the table to deliver it to her brother who she knew loved homemade whipped cream. The whole scene was so bighearted and beautiful. What more could a mother want?

Wait.

On her way around the table, my helpful girl slipped. She landed on her bottom with a thud. The glass bowl shattered, and the homemade whipped cream flew everywhere. Oh, how she cried for so many reasons. Her brother was crushed because of the tragic death of the whipped cream. And I suddenly noticed twelve bare feet hovering dangerously close to the shards of glass on the floor. I also noticed that it was 8:15 a.m.

Beautiful, good-smelling moments seemed to teeter on stilts that were repeatedly knocked out from under me.

If the day was going to progress smoothly, we needed to finish breakfast and begin our Morning Time by eight thirty. I sighed. Plan A wasn't going to happen—again.

Anger burned inside me. I hadn't slept through the night in fifteen years, and I was exhausted. Sudden emergencies like this had occurred every day for as long as I could remember. Beautiful, good-smelling moments seemed to teeter on stilts that were repeatedly knocked out from under me. I had lost my temper over situations just like this one many times in the past.

Depression tugged on me too. I often felt invisible—worthless—only good for cleaning up messes or keeping the peace. When the tyranny of the urgent, as they say, kept me from completing any meaningful work, I easily lost my footing and sank into depression.

I stood in the middle of the mess, searching for the fruit of the Spirit in my soul. Where was joy? Where was peace? Where was patience? I felt as if God's good gifts to mothers had gone up in smoke. As anger and depression bore down on me, I begged the Holy Spirit for help, and He reminded me of an important truth I had been learning for quite some time.

SERVING WITH GREAT JOY

Several years earlier, I had heard a radio series honoring Vonette Bright. Vonette and her husband, Bill Bright, lived long, fruitful lives, raising two sons and cofounding Campus Crusade for Christ—now CRU—a college-based ministry that has shared the good news of Christ with countless people all over the world. Vonette had recently passed away, and the ministry Revive Our Hearts was celebrating her life by airing a series of interviews she had given over the years. I'm so encouraged at these glimpses of the lives of those who have gone on before us.

In one interview, Vonette was in her seventies. Her husband, Bill, had been diagnosed with pulmonary fibrosis, a lung disease that would take his life not many weeks later. Several of Vonette's friends had recently died and she, too, was beginning to face some of the effects of aging. She was in a season of life where she could reflect on what matters most in life. In the interview, her voice is strong and confident as she talks about her salvation, devotional life, and her love for her husband and their two sons. One part especially had an impact on me as a mom: the host, Nancy DeMoss Wolgemuth, asks, "If you could give a single word of counsel, wisdom, advice ... what would you say to us?"

Without skipping a beat, Vonette replies,

> Well, the first thing that comes to mind is serve the Lord with gladness, and just give yourself in total abandonment to Him. Whether you're single, whether you're

married, whether you have children, whatever ages your children are, do it all to the honor of God and just serve Him with gladness. . . . God doesn't want us to work for Him; He wants to do His work in and through us. As we make ourselves available to Him, allow the Holy Spirit to control our lives from the top of our head to the tip of our toe, then He's going to do what He wishes to do through us. That will be serving the Lord with gladness.[20]

This was not what I expected. Vonette Bright had traveled all over the world and knew lots of people, important people. She had a relationship with the Lord and a ministry I would love to have, and yet her single word of wisdom from a life well lived was simply, "Serve the LORD with gladness!" (This gem is found in Psalm 100:2.)

In the next interview, Vonette is much older and mere weeks away from dying. Her beloved husband had gone to be with the Lord years earlier. In this interview, you can hear her longing for heaven: she is ready to meet Jesus. At one point in the interview, Vonette reflects on her life, saying, "I'm grateful for what God's allowed me to do. It's all been His doing. I've served Him with great joy. He's honored my efforts far beyond anything I could ever understand."[21] Amazed, I heard the same theme from the previous interview: "I've served him with great joy."

At the end of her life, with eighty-nine years under her belt, Vonette was still holding on to the value of serving the Lord with gladness. I took it to heart. God knew I needed to hear His encouragement every day as I raised my children. He stirred my spirit with it as if He were saying, "Serve the Lord with gladness, Laura. I'll help you do it." Psalm 100:2 became my anthem.

THE BEAUTIFUL BROKEN BOWL

A couple of years after hearing that interview, we welcomed our sixth baby. She was so kissable and utterly adorable, but going from five to six children—especially while homeschooling—overwhelmed me. No amount of strategizing or simplifying seemed to put a dent in the physical workload or the mental and emotional investment of serving around the clock. I loved our precious children with all my heart, but I was in over my head. Every day, I prayed for God's practical, in-the-moment help. Every day, I heard the Lord cheer me on. "Serve the Lord with gladness, Laura," but to tell you the truth, I struggled to do it.

As I struggled, I sensed the Holy Spirit urging me to sing. When my workload loomed like a mountain, and the kids were squabbling, and a dozen urgent needs vied for my attention, the Holy Spirit seemed to be saying to me, "Sing! Sing! Sing!" Well, wouldn't you know, in those moments, I couldn't think of a song. Not "Jesus Loves Me," not "Amazing Grace," not "The Wheels on the Bus," not one single song came to mind. I reached out to my friend Brea, saying, "I need a song to sing when daily things go wrong like a glass breaks or a child gets hurt. Do you have any suggestions?" Brea wrote back with a link to Chris Tomlin's

"Everlasting God." This helped. (Check it out—you'll love it!)

Miraculously, when I was in the blur of serving my family, I could recall Brea's suggestion, and I could sing. Each time, the Lord worked through the song to transform my anger and depression into gladness. One day, I realized the connection between Vonette's advice to "serve the Lord with gladness," and the Holy Spirit's nudge to "sing!" As it turns out, the entirety of Psalm 100:2 is, "Serve the LORD with gladness! Come into his presence with singing!" Sometimes, it's just that the second part has to come first.

The Lord brought all of this to my mind that day my little girl fell with a thud and the whipped cream flew everywhere. My soul felt devoid of spiritual fruit, but I knew God had established this work for me and He would carry me through. I carefully moved each barefoot child to safety and hugged my daughter. As I picked up each glass shard and wiped up the whipped cream, I decided to sing to Jesus. I knew He was there with me in my exhaustion and discouragement. It was a humble moment—after all, cleaning up whipped cream is no big deal in light of the world's problems—but God met me in an everyday catastrophe, rescued me from myself, and turned my eyes toward Jesus. How very kind.

As I picked up each glass shard and wiped up the whipped cream, I decided to sing to Jesus. I knew He was there with me in my exhaustion and discouragement.

Afterward, I gathered the kids in the living room for our Morning Time. I usually looked ahead at the morning's Bible reading and prepared something tangible to help the kids connect with the text. (Nothing fancy, but for example, the day we read, "Jesus declared, 'I am the bread of life,'" we ate bread.) On this particular day, I hadn't had time to look ahead, so I just opened my Bible to John 12 and began reading where we had left off the day before, in verse 3: the story of Mary of Bethany anointing Jesus at a dinner party.

> *Mary therefore took a pound of expensive ointment made from pure nard, and anointed the feet of Jesus and wiped his feet with her hair. The house was filled with the fragrance of the perfume.*

Matthew tells the same story in his gospel (see 26:8–13) and specifies,

> *When the disciples saw it, they were indignant, saying, "Why this waste? For this could have been sold for a large sum and given to the poor." But Jesus, aware of this, said to them . . . "She has done a beautiful thing to me. . . . In pouring this ointment on my body, she has done it to prepare me for burial. Truly, I say to you, wherever this gospel is proclaimed in the whole world, what she has done will also be told in memory of her."*

My jaw dropped. Even my youngest children saw the parallels of Mary's valuable jar of perfume, broken and wasted. They exclaimed, "Us too! We had a bowl of something precious and it was broken and wasted all over the floor." (God plans the best hands-on Bible lessons.)

I love this story about Mary and what it reveals about her faith. She had heard Jesus talk about His pending death, burial, and resurrection, and this was her opportunity to demonstrate that she believed Him. In anointing Jesus for burial with her expensive perfume, Mary was saying, "Yes, Jesus. Go to the cross." She must have felt the urgency of His atoning death: she herself was broken, and she lived in a broken world. She needed a Savior to stoop down, gather the pieces together, and make all things new.

• • •

You and I need a Savior to stoop down and meet us in our brokenness too. We are derailed by brokenness on every side. It may be simple like a shattered bowl of whipped cream or more grievous like a besetting sin, a difficult child, or a chronic illness. God sees us when we are standing in the middle of a mess, wondering what we should do next. He flies to our side and gets to work, comforting, restoring, and strengthening us. But what is more, Jesus promises to return to earth and create a world where people and things don't break anymore.

> *No longer will there be anything accursed, but the throne of God and of the Lamb will be in it, and his servants will worship him. They will see his face, and his name will be on their foreheads. And night will be no more. They will need no light of lamp or sun, for the Lord God will be their light, and they will reign forever and ever.—Revelation 22:3–5*

The next-to-last verse in the Bible has Jesus promising, "Surely I am coming soon" (Rev. 22:20). Every day, you and I are invited to anoint His feet with the offering of a worshipful heart, and say, "Yes. Come, Lord Jesus!" We have opportunities like Mary's to demonstrate our faith that He will do what He says He will do.

Whenever we stoop to clean a mess, answer a crisis, or enter someone else's brokenness, we are saying, "Yes, Jesus. Come renew this world." Whenever we clean up the kitchen, organize a child's bedroom, or pray about a child's broken heart, we are saying, "Yes, Jesus. Come renew this world." Whenever we serve the Lord with gladness and come into His presence with singing, we are saying, "Yes. Come, Lord Jesus." And He will. Soon.

Even when there is no sign of fruit in our lives, we have good reason to worship God, for we have Jesus, our beloved Savior, Shepherd, and Friend. We will share the good news with the next generation so they might know Him and praise Him too.

RECEIVING COUNTLESS OPPORTUNITIES TO WORSHIP

Something to cherish:
Make a joyful noise to the LORD, all the earth! Serve the LORD with gladness! Come into his presence with singing!—Psalm 100:1–2

Something to sing:
"We Will Feast in the House of Zion" by Sandra McCracken

Something to read:
Adorned: Living Out the Beauty of the Gospel Together by Nancy DeMoss Wolgemuth

Something to consider:

- In what areas of my life am I called to serve today?

- How can I open the door to more gladness as I serve in these areas?

- Will I trust Jesus to take my service, poured out and given to Him at His feet, as an act of worship?

- What song can I sing when my heart is cold and I need to be reminded of His great love for me?

MY PRAYER FOR YOU: *May you have faith to believe that Jesus is with you in the brokenness and that He will come again to make all things new. Until then, may your life be a fragrant offering to Him as you serve Him in big and small ways.*

Whenever you must clean up literal brokenness or tend to spiritual or relational brokenness, may you see it for what it is: an opportunity to serve the Lord with gladness. And when you can't see a hint of fruit on the vine and all seems lost, may you worship Jesus all the more, knowing that Christ has you and He is all you need.

POSTSCRIPT

This past weekend, we tucked our youngest into a "big girl bed" for the first time. She's sharing a room with her big sisters now and she is tickled pink about it. We moved the crib out of the nursery and slid our computer desk into its place. Just like that, the tiny nursery transformed into an office where I am writing this postscript.

Before we overhauled the space, I sat in the rocking chair, studying the empty crib and thanking God for the time I have spent here with my children. My babies needed me to be here with them. Every morning, I opened the blinds to let the sunshine in. I fed them. Changed them. Played with them. Every evening, I dimmed the lights and said goodnight.

Looking back, I can see that I needed them to be here with me too. I needed them to show me what it looks like to be human. I needed them to lay their whole weight on me, feed from my body, and rely on me. I needed them to pull me away from the hustle and bustle and give me no other choice but to stay in this hushed and holy space with them. I needed them to teach me how to focus on one person at a time and to be completely devoted. And I needed them to love me simply because I was their mom. They chose my smell, my shape, my temperature, my voice, and my face over everyone else's in the world. I'll cherish this forever.

In this space, my children taught me about God. I'd peek in on them as they slept. Sometimes, fearing the worst, I'd tentatively place my hand on their back or under their nose to feel the steady rise and fall of their breath. For every countless undeserved moment when all was well, I thanked God for keeping the frailest humans alive despite everything they're up against.

"Thank You, heavenly Father. In this nursery, You have loved and nurtured me."

> *Motherhood isn't a story about our evolution to greatness: it's a story about God's greatness toward us.*

You might remember that our nursery started out as a place of desolation and lost hope. On moving day, we walked the crib past the doorway and didn't stop until it was hidden in the attic. Little did we know, we would bring the crib back down and fill it with four more precious babies. Each of our children has blessed me far more than I expected when I first told Ryan I wanted to be a mom someday. I certainly didn't anticipate this turn of events—of me writing to you about them in the very space—the very square foot—where so much of my motherhood journey has happened so far.

I'm letting myself cry tonight, knowing I must roll up my

sleeves and get to work tomorrow: I have teenagers to love, middle-schoolers to enjoy, and little ones who still need hugs, snacks, and naps. Thankfully, I have friends like you to journey alongside.

So, what can you and I expect from motherhood? When I ask older moms for their thoughts on the matter, I hear a resounding answer no matter how things turned out for themselves or their kids: "It was all God's grace and all for His glory."

I think what they're saying is that motherhood isn't about our evolution to greatness: it's about God's greatness toward us. It isn't about how we got everything right, but how Christ did, for us. It isn't about discovering work-life balance, parenting formulas, or how to be a supermom: it's about Jesus, our Good Shepherd, who draws us close to His side when we need Him most, holds our kids close to His heart, and guides us all the way home. I see this golden thread woven throughout my story so far. Do you see glimmers of it in yours too?

I can't help but wonder what life will look like beyond "the little years" without pregnancy, newborns, and toddlers. Thinking about my children growing up and moving out into the world boggles my mind. The future feels strange and unknown. But after writing this book, I know that the same God who has been with me during these early years of motherhood will be with me—and with you—in the future too. At the end of our motherhood journeys, I expect you and I will smile and repeat the same predictable conclusion as every woman who has walked this path by Jesus' side: *It was all God's grace and all for His glory.*

How beautiful.

ACKNOWLEDGMENTS

Thank you, dear friends:

Brea, Renee, Chizzy, and Amber for reading early chapters and joining me in prayer about this book.

Kaela and Maggie for taking my hand and helping me to jump into this project.

Amy and Molly for daydreaming with me about my children when we were children ourselves.

Lois, for your kindness and wisdom all along the way.

And to every friend who has loved and strengthened me over the years, thank you. Thank you.

Thank you to those who literally made this book better:

Brea Asbury and Renee Behringer for contributing to the "Something to consider" prompts.

Dannah Gresh, Erin Davis, Heather Holleman, Suzie D'Souza, and Laura Fabrycky for professional advice and good cheer.

Judy Dunagan, Pam Pugh, and the hardworking team at Moody Publishers. Working with you has been a delight, and I'm grateful to each person who has contributed to this endeavor.

Pastor Dan Kiehl for your careful reading of this book and your shepherding over the years.

Thank you to my family who has loved and served me without limit:

Bob and Eileen, my mother- and father-in-law.

Heather, Jared, and Evan.

Julie, Erin, and Emily, my sisters—and their husbands and all their delightful children.

Mom and Dad, my foundation in life and the wind at my back.

Thank you to Vivienne, Lia, Juliette, Malachi, Audrey, Josiah, and Gretl. You are precious to me and I love you. You helped me write this book and it is yours.

Thank you, Ryan. For everything. I love you.

And, most of all, thank You, Jesus, for holding us close to Your heart. *It's all for You.*

NOTES

1. C. S. Lewis, *Mere Christianity* (New York: Touchstone, 1996), 153.
2. Paul David Tripp, *New Morning Mercies: A Daily Gospel Devotional* (Wheaton, IL: Crossway, 2014), July 23.
3. This quote has been traced to Ellen Cantarow, "No Kids," in the *Village Voice* (1985) and used in a slightly different form by Elizabeth Stone, who credits Cantarow with its origin (Tom Krazit, "The Backstory of Steve Jobs' Quote about Parenthood," GigaOm, October 11, 2011, https://gigaom.com/2011/10/11/419-the-long-backstory-of-steve-jobs-quote-about-parenthood/).
4. Nancy Guthrie, *The One Year Praying through the Bible for Your Kids* (Carol Stream, IL: Tyndale House Publishers, 2016), xii.
5. Facing bouts of infertility for several years, I often struggled with taking too many pregnancy tests. I finally confided in my husband. He understood. Then he proposed a plan: we purchased four tests each month and kept them in the bathroom

closet where we both could see them. I took a test every Friday morning whether I felt like I may be pregnant or not. This gave me some healthy accountability as well as peace of mind that a test was coming. Ryan knew when I needed extra care as I grappled with the negative results. If you can relate to this part of my story, please know I included it specifically for you. My heart goes out to you and I understand.

6. I'm grateful to Pastor Benjamin Lee for permission to use these three statements, borrowed from his sermon "Mercy Reigns" on Habakkuk 3:1–16, August 9, 2020.

7. *The Valley of Vision* (Carlisle, PA: The Banner of Truth Trust, 1975), 75.

8. "Malcolm Gladwell: Talking to Strangers," *Oprah's Super Soul Conversations*, Omny.fm, September 18, 2019, https://omny.fm/shows/oprah-s-supersoul-conversations/malcolm-gladwell-talking-to-strangers.

9. John Owen, *The Works of John Owen, Vol. 3: The Holy Spirit* (Carlisle, PA: Banner of Truth, 1996), 108–9.

10. *The Valley of Vision*, 25.

11. Alistair Begg, "Justice and Love," Truth For Life, April 14, 2006, https://www.truthforlife.org/resources/sermon/justice-and-love/. (The italicized phrases in this section come from this sermon.)

12. Called the Serenity Prayer, these lines are often attributed to Protestant theologian Reinhold Niebuhr, but its origin is, in fact, unknown.

13. Corrie ten Boom, *Jesus Is Victor* (Grand Rapids: Revell, 1984).

14. John Piper, "How Do You Define Joy?," Desiring God, July 15, 2016, https://www.desiringgod.org/articles/how-do-you-define-joy.

15. Heather Holleman, *Seated with Christ: Living Freely in a Culture of Comparison* (Chicago: Moody, 2015), 128.

16. Elisabeth Elliot, *Passion and Purity: Learning to Bring Your Love Life under Christ's Control* (Grand Rapids, MI: Revell, 1984), 89.

17. Quote from American writer Henry James, https://quote investigator.com/2018/09/21/kind/.

18. This quote has been attributed to Thomas à Kempis, a Roman Catholic monk who lived around 1380–1471 and is well known for his classic work *The Imitation of Christ*.

19. Sally Clarkson, *Own Your Life: Living with Deep Intention, Bold Faith, and Generous Love* (Carol Stream, IL: Tyndale House Publishers, 2014), 50.

20. "Remembering Vonette Bright, Day 2," *Revive Our Hearts* podcast, February 2, 2016, https://www.reviveourhearts.com/ podcast/revive-our-hearts/remembering-vonette-bright-day-2/.

21. "Remembering Vonette Bright, Day 3," *Revive Our Hearts* podcast, February 3, 2016, https://www.reviveourhearts.com/ podcast/revive-our-hearts/remembering-vonette-bright-day-3/.